Stories
of
Christmas Carols

Also by the author

Stories of Yuletide
Living Stories of Famous Hymns
Famous Stories of Inspiring Hymns
40 Stories of Famous Gospel Songs
Stories of Songs about Heaven
Hymn Stories for Programs
Popular Programs Based on Hymn Stories

Stories
of
Christmas Carols

Ernest K. Emurian

Baker Books
A Division of Baker Book House Co.
Grand Rapids, Michigan 49516

© 1958, 1967 by Baker Book House Company

Published by Baker Books
a division of Baker Book House Company
P.O. Box 6287, Grand Rapids, MI 49516-6287

Cloth edition published 1996

Third printing, July 1998

Printed in the United States of America

ISBN 0-8010-1136-1
Library of Congress Catalog Card Number 58-12415

For information about new releases available from Baker Book House, visit our web site:
http://www.bakerbooks.com/

To
My Mother
whose singing of Isaac Watts'
cradle song
"Hush, My Dear, Lie Still and Slumber"
is
one of the earliest recollections
of
my childhood.

PREFACE

Henry Kirk White (1785-1806) was possibly the youngest hymn-writer to pen a popular poem about Christmas. The first stanza of his hymn (which is sometimes known by the opening line of the second stanza, "Once on the raging seas I rode"), contains these lines:

When marshalled on the nightly plain The glittering host
    bestud the sky,
One star alone of all the train Can fix the sinner's wander-
    ing eye;
Hark, hark, to God the chorus breaks From every host, from
    every gem,
But one alone the Saviour speaks, It is the Star of Bethle-
    hem.

The oldest Christmas poet was, undoubtedly, the brilliant American literary giant, William Cullen Bryant (1794-1878). Although he penned "Thanatopsis" when he was a youth of nineteen, he did not write his Advent hymn until he was eighty-one, and the only reason he wrote it at all was because he was requested to do so for the semi-centennial celebration of Boston's Church of the Messiah. Bryant took as his subject matter the same theme which had intrigued White in England three quarters of a century earlier, and wrote two stanzas, the second of which was this:

*Yet doth the Star of Bethlehem shed A lustre pure and
sweet,*
And still it leads, as once it led, To the Messiah's feet.
O Father, may that holy star Grow every year more bright,
*And send its glorious beams afar To fill the world with
light.*

The rest of the great Advent poets did their
creative work between their nineteenth and
eighty-first years, writing hymns, songs and
carols for the glory of God and the education,
enrichment and entertainment of their fellow
men.

ERNEST K. EMURIAN
Cherrydale Methodist Church
Arlington, Virginia

CONTENTS

Chapter I

ANGELS FROM THE REALMS
OF GLORY

ANGELS FROM THE REALMS
OF GLORY

In the story of newspaper editor James Mont-gomery it was not a case of from rags to riches but rather from prison cell to first citizen of Sheffield, England. His boyhood days would hardly be characterized as happy or successful ones, even though his piously devout Moravian parents reared him in the cultured Christian at-mosphere of a happy home. When they sailed for the West Indies as foreign missionaries dur-ing little James' sixth year, the lad was placed in an institution that proved to be more of a monastery than a boarding-school, and, after his parents' death at their mission post, the boy was shunted hither and yon in a manner that would have crushed the spirit of a less deter-mined or less devout youth. The heritage of hymn singing, both at home and at school, stood the boy in good stead in later years, since it eventually fired the spark of creative genius that lingered in his soul. He tried his own hand at writing poetry as early as his tenth year, and, in his early teens, packed up his few belongings, tucked his precious manuscript under his arm and went to London in high hopes of finding a pub-

lisher for his book of original poems. The bitter
memories of failure at school and several months
as a baker's apprentice, as well as homelessness
and general loneliness spurred him on, and although he failed to find a publisher, he sold one
of his poems to a kind-hearted man whom he
persuaded to buy with a gift of salesmanship that
belied his youthful appearance and years.

The purchaser was generous enough with his
money, however, to stake the teen-ager until he
could find a steady, if not a lucrative, job. At
twenty-one, when he answered an ad for a helper
on the staff of the radical newspaper "The Sheffield Register," James found the position for
which he felt all of his previous experiences had
prepared him.

When the editor of the paper planned to flee
the country to escape threatened prosecution for
some of his critical editorials and articles, young
Montgomery (1771-1854) bought him out, re-
named the paper "The Iris" and embarked upon
what he thought would be a glorious career as a
newspaperman. But it was a prison cell rather
than the plaudits of the citizens that awaited him.
France was in the midst of her bloody revolution,
and, while Britain and France were nominally
at peace, the British were trying to raise an army
for what they considered an inevitable war with
their neighbour across the English Channel once
the Revolution was over. While the British gov-

ernment claimed to be neutral, His Majesty's
subjects had already taken sides, rallying to the
support of the French people who, they felt, were
justified in taking up arms against a decadent
and corrupt government.

Montgomery printed in the columns of "The
Sheffield Iris" a rather inflammatory poem celebrating the fall of the Bastille in Paris at the
hands of a French mob, and soon found himself
before the bar of justice in the local court house
on the grounds of having unduly incited the
British people to take sides with regard to the
internal affairs of France. The twenty-three-
year-old poet-turned-editor could offer no objec-
tion or defense other than the very obvious fact
that the people had taken sides whether His Majesty's government wished to admit the fact or not.
The judge, however, saw his duty and did it, sen-
tencing Montgomery to three months in the local
jail, in addition to a fine of twenty pounds ($100).
Off to prison the young man went, thinking possibly that his erstwhile employer, Mr. Gales, had
shown far more wisdom in skipping the country
than staying to face the music. But his friends
rallied to his support, raised his fine, and bailed
him out, little the worse for his brief incarcera-
tion. If some conservative townsmen thought the
experience had taught the brash editor a lesson,
and that he would hew to the political straight
and narrow from then on, they were sadly mis-

taken, because, two years later, Montgomery found himself again in hot water for carrying in his paper a rather detailed account of a working-man's riot in a local mill. Considering his newspaper story "inimical to the public interest," the judge this time doubled the jail sentence to six months and jumped the fine to $150. Having learned his lesson two years earlier, the editor devoted this period of confinement to writing a book, which he entitled "Prison Amusements." When he stepped out a free man six months later, he was surprised to discover that he had become something of a celebrity, that his first book had become a best-seller and that the circulation of "The Sheffield Iris" was larger than ever before in its history.

So famous had he become, in fact, that he was almost tempted to write the local judge a letter of thanks for having afforded him the privilege of the second prison experience! Using his growing influence, not only as a bold and gifted writer, but also as a devout and consistent Christian, Montgomery began to devote his time and talents to creative writing, championing many varied and unpopular causes, from foreign missions to the abolition of the slave trade and from humanizing the lot of the chimney-sweeps to encouraging the widespread use of the Holy Bible.

Maturing and mellowing with the years, he grew in stature and stability and by his fortieth birthday was generally recognized as the leading citizen of his city. Like the pioneer editor-poet, Joseph Addison, who published many of his original poems in the columns of "The Spectator," James Montgomery began to include some of his original poems in the columns of "The Iris." Noting the enthusiastic response which greeted these works, he was encouraged to devote more and more of his energy and ability to the writing of hymns. As a close and careful student of the Holy Scripture, he was reading once again the familiar story of the birth of Jesus preparatory to writing an article for the Christmas Eve edition of his paper in 1816, his forty-fifth year. Inspired by the age-old account of the advent of the infant King, the visit of the shepherds and the sages and saints, as well as the angel song which heralded and welcomed the miracle of love, the poet penned five stanzas, subsequently reduced to four, the first of which read:

Angels from the realms of glory, Wing your flight o'er all the earth;
Ye who sang creation's story, Now proclaim Messiah's birth:
Come and worship, Come and worship,
Worship Christ the new-born King.

Published in the December 24, 1816 issue of "The Iris," this poem was picked up and included in the 1819 edition of Cotterill's "Selection." The poet himself, after revising a few of his lines, included it in one of his own books, "Christian Psalmist," six years later, in 1825.

The stirring tune, "Regent Square," to which this hymn is now universally sung, came from the pen of the blind musician-composer, Henry Smart (1813-1879), taking its name from the most prominent Presbyterian Church in London, Regent Square Church, being given that name by the minister of the congregation at the time he included the hymn and new tune in "Psalms and Hymns for Divine Worship," dated 1867. Smart also composed the tune "Lancashire" (Lead On, O King Eternal) about 1835, and the tune "Pilgrims" (Hark, Hark My Soul) in 1868.

Five years after he had penned this majestic Advent hymn, Montgomery was inspired to prepare a metrical version of Psalm Seventy-Two that many poets and hymnologists agree was the finest thing he ever wrote. This psalm, which inspired Isaac Watts to write the first great missionary hymn in the English language, "Jesus Shall Reign Where'er The Sun," first published in 1719, became the background against which Montgomery, a little over a century later, wrote his Christmas hymn which began:

Hail to the Lord's Anointed, Great David's greater Son!
Hail in the time appointed His work on earth begun!
He comes to break oppression, To set the captive free,
To take away transgression And rule in equity.

While the poet declared that, in writing this hymn, "his hand trembled to touch the harp of Zion," following its first public use at a service in an English Moravian center at Fulneck on Christmas Day, December 25, 1821, it was widely used, even being included in Dr. Adam Clark's monumental "Commentary" at the insistence of Clark himself.

Many of the reforms for which Montgomery fought were gradually adopted by the British government, and, in gratitude to the talented poet, hymn writer and fiery editor, he was given a liberal annual royal pension from 1833 until his death twenty-one years later. He bought a palatial home, "The Mount," located on the highest piece of land in Sheffield, and lived there for many years, being respected and honored as the "first citizen" of the city.

As an author, he produced more than four hundred hymns, as well as numerous books on a wide variety of subjects, and today he ranks among the most popular hymn writers of the Christian era, being surpassed only by Charles Wesley and Isaac Watts in the number of hymns now in general use throughout Christendom. Among his best hymns are "Prayer Is The Soul's Sincere Desire," "In The Hour Of Trial," "God Is My Strong Salvation" and "The Lord Is My Shepherd, No Want Shall I Know."

With Wesley and Dix, this devout Moravian

has the honor of having two Christmas hymns accepted by Christians throughout the world, a worthy testimony to his noble character, his knowledge of the Holy Scripture and his poetic ability.

ANGELS FROM THE REALMS OF GLORY

*Angels from the realms of glory, Wing your flight o'er all
    the earth;*
*Ye who sang creation's story, Now proclaim Messiah's
    birth;*
*Come and worship, Come and worship, Worship Christ the
    new-born King.*

*Shepherds in the field abiding, Watching o'er your flocks
    by night,*
*God with man is now residing; Yonder shines the infant
    light;*
*Come and worship, Come and worship, Worship Christ the
    new-born King.*

*Sages, leave your contemplations, Brighter visions beam
    afar;*
*Seek the great Desire of nations; Ye have seen his natal
    star;*
*Come and worship, Come and worship, Worship Christ the
    new-born King.*

*Saints, before the altar bending, Watching long in hope and
    fear,*
Suddenly the Lord descending In his temple shall appear;
*Come and worship, Come and worship, Worship Christ the
    new-born King.*

*Sinners, wrung with true repentance, Doomed for guilt to
    endless pains,*
*Justice now revokes the sentence; Mercy calls you, break
    your chains.*
*Come and worship, Come and worship, Worship Christ the
    new-born King.*

HAIL TO THE LORD'S ANNOINTED

(In this version, stanzas 4 and 5 of the original 7 are
omitted, while the first half of stanza 6 is coupled with the
second half of stanza 7 to make stanza 4.)

Hail to the Lord's annointed, Great David's greater Son!
Hail, in the time appointed, His reign on earth begun!
He comes to break oppression, To set the captive free,
To take away transgression, And rule in equity.

He comes with succor speedy, To those who suffer wrong;
To help the poor and needy And bid the weak be strong:
To give them songs for sighing, Their darkness turn to light,
*Whose souls, condemned and dying, Were precious in his
    sight.*

He shall descend like showers Upon the fruitful earth,
And love and joy like flowers Spring in his path to birth:
Before him on the mountains, Shall peace the herald go,
And righteousness in fountains From hill to valley flow.

For him shall prayer unceasing And daily vows ascend:
His kingdom still increasing, A kingdom without end.
The tide of time shall never His covenant remove:
His name shall stand forever, His great, best name of Love.

Chapter II

AS WITH GLADNESS MEN OF OLD

AS WITH GLADNESS MEN OF OLD

It is likely that William Chatterton Dix (1837-1898) wrote both of his famous Christmas carols on the same day, although this would be as difficult to prove as to disprove. However, since both of them were inspired by the same passage of Scripture, and both deal with the same subject matter, it is not hard to believe that both were written on Epiphany Day, 1859, a few months prior to the poet's twenty-second birthday.

Dix, the son of an eminent surgeon of Bristol, England, was born in that city in June, 1837. In later years he said rather boastfully, "I was born the year in which Morse invented the telegraph and the year that Queen Victoria ascended the throne of the British Empire." Despite the high esteem in which his physician father was held by the citizens of Bristol, young William showed little inclination to follow Dr. William Dix's footsteps. After finishing his studies in the city's Grammar School, the young man felt the irresistible siren call of the business world, whereupon he moved to Glasgow, Scotland, and began selling insurance. When friends asked, "Why did you not follow your father's profession and take up the study of medicine?" the young salesman replied, "Medicine is not for me. I am a business man at heart and have neither the desire nor the inclination to become a physician or a surgeon. Insurance is my line, and I cannot think of anything worse than forcing a man who wants to sell insurance to enter the medical profession unless it is compelling a man who wants to become a doctor to take up the selling of insurance."

That generally silenced the critical and the curious who thought it rather strange for a young man to turn his back upon a lucrative professional career for the rough and tumble struggle of the business world. He did follow his distinguished father in one respect, however, for both father and son became well-known authors. The elder Dix wrote a successful biography of another of Bristol's famous sons, Lord Chatterton, his regard for the subject of the book being evident in the fact that he gave His Lordship's last name to his own son as a middle name. The younger Dix wrote several volumes of poetry, his first successful book, "Hymns Of Love And Joy," being published in 1861, in addition to several collections of translations of Greek and Abyssinian hymns and sacred poems. "I've taken up the study of Greek and Ethiopian," he told his pastor one day, "in order to be able to translate some of our hymns into those languages and to translate some of their finest literary masterpieces into our own tongue. After all, there are some excellent hymns in the languages of both of those people and it would greatly enrich their worship if they would use our noblest hymns in their tongue while it would mean almost as much to us if we could sing their hymns in our language in turn."

Despite his father's watchful care, young William suffered two periods of prolonged illness between his twenty-first and his thirtieth birthdays, and it was during the long days of confinement brought about by these times of ill-health that he produced several of the poetic gems with which his name will forever be associated and by means of which his memory will be perpetuated. Since languishing in bed is persecution to a person with an active mind, despite the pains the body may be suffering, the young insurance man began a careful study of the New Testament, reading over and over again many of the passages he knew almost by heart, in an effort to discover some hidden meaning that had escaped him heretofore. Thus it was that on Epiphany Day, 1859, he read once more the assigned lesson, being an obedient and dutiful High Churchman (Anglican), and suddenly, as he went over the familiar verses in Matthew 2:1-12, the story of the visit of the wise men took on new meaning. As a faithful Churchman, he knew all of the traditions that had grown up around that particular story through the years, especially the one which described the three "Kings" as the spiritual successors to the three sons of Noah: Shem, Ham and Japheth; and the other one which named and described them in this manner: Melchior was an old man with beautiful long white hair and a flowing beard to match, who brought a gift of gold, worthy of a King, while Caspar was a beardless youth of ruddy complexion who presented a gift of frankincense as to a Deity, while dark-skinned and swarthy Balthasar carried myrrh for the Lord's burial. He smiled as he recalled a sermon in which a brother had declared that the three wise men or Kings represented the three ages of man: youth, manhood and maturity, basing his assumption on the tradition that one of the Magi was a youth, another a young man and the third an aged person, all of which had no basis whatsoever in the Biblical account of their visit as recorded in Matthew's Gospel.

When Dix discovered that a twelfth century ecclesiastic, Bishop Reinald of Cologne, Germany, claimed to have found the skulls of the three wise men which he exhibited to all of the faithful in his diocese who could pay the required fee, he knew that the Scripture story in all of its simplicity was closer to the truth. That night he said to his father, "This business of three kings from the orient just is not true. It is merely part of the tradition that grew up around the birth of Our Lord and has no Biblical basis whatsoever." Explaining to his curious parent that the tradition of the three kings grew up because of the three gifts the eastern travellers gave to the Christ Child, he told him that he had recently completed a new hymn on the subject which made no reference whatsoever to the wise men, Magi or Kings.

Dr. Dix, pleased that such an interest indicated an improvement in the condition of his favorite patient, urged his son to read some of his newly written stanzas. "My curiosity is getting the best of me, William," his father said. "Read what you have written." Whereupon William, complying with the older man's request, read the first stanza of his new hymn:

As with gladness men of old, Did the guiding star behold;
As with joy they hailed its light, Leading onward, beaming
    bright;
So most gracious Lord, may we Evermore be led to Thee.

"I see you referred to the easterners as 'men' instead of 'wise men,' 'Magi' or 'Kings,' " Dr. Dix said.

"I did it on purpose, Father," the youth explained, "so no one could challenge the authenticity of my statement. They were men; at least we can all agree on that." His father nodded as he added, "I like the conclusion which you drew at the close of the stanza, son. Too many European carols are merely descriptive poems that contain no convincing statement regarding what we are supposed to do about the birth of Jesus."

Dix's second stanza originally began with these words:

As with joyful steps they sped To that Lowly manger bed.

Later, remembering that the oriental visitors "went into the house" in Bethlehem where "they saw the young child with Mary his mother," he was tempted to change the line to read:

As with joyful steps they sped To the Saviour's lowly bed,

so his readers would know that they did not actually go to the manger in the stable but to the house in which the holy family was staying following the Lord's birth. But it is his original that has stood the test of time and is in general use today. He even left the reference to the "manger" in the third stanza, although he did not mention either the names or the number of the gifts they brought. The first four of his original five stanzas comprise the carol as we know it today, and a more general hymn on such a specific theme would be difficult to find.

Since his other popular carol is undated, but

is connected with the Feast of the Epiphany also, it could have been inspired the same day by the reading of the same familiar story. This hymn is known by its opening phrase, "What child is this?" as well as by the fact that it is now sung to an old English tune commonly called "Greensleeves," a piece of music popular in Shakespeare's day which became a hymn tune after the famous nineteenth century composer, Sir John Stainer, harmonized it during the last century. In this carol, Dix has the infant Jesus "Where ox and ass are feeding," and he lists the three gifts without mentioning "men," "Magi" or the "Kings," but the outstanding feature of his poem lies in the fact that he refers to the Lord's death as well as His birth in the second stanza,

Nails, spear, shall pierce Him through, The cross be borne for me, for you.

And, as in his earlier carol, he does not hesitate to tell believers what is expected of them in view of the gift of God to sinful man.

Dix's illness in 1867 led him to find new meaning in the Great Invitation of Jesus, "Come unto me, all ye that labor and are heavy laden, and I will give you rest" (Matthew 11:28), as a result of which he wrote the hymn, "Come Unto Me, Ye Weary, And I Will Give You Rest." An almost miraculous recovery of health followed the completion of this hymn which led the poet to say, "I always look back to that hymn as the turning point in my illness."

The last of his four books of poems, "Seekers Of A City," was published in 1878, twenty-years before his death at the age of sixty-one. The future of hymnody is secure as long as any Church can produce a layman like Dix at least once every generation. The Anglican Communion can well be proud of him, since his two Christmas hymns rank with the best of Watts and Wesley, not only in the hymnals of Christendom but also in the hearts of the people.

As with Gladness Men of Old

As with gladness men of old Did the guiding star behold;
As with joy they hailed its light, Leading onward, beaming
    bright;
So, most gracious Lord, may we Evermore be led to thee.

As with joyful steps they sped To that lowly manger bed,
There to bend the knee before Him whom heaven and earth
    adore;
So may we with willing feet Ever seek thy mercy-seat.

As they offered gifts most rare At that manger rude and
    bare;
So may we with holy joy, Pure and free from sin's alloy,
All our costliest treasures bring, Christ, to thee, our
    heavenly King.

Holy Jesus, every day Keep us in the narrow way;
And, when earthly things are past, Bring our ransomed
souls at last
Where they need no star to guide, Where no clouds thy
glory hide.

In the heavenly country bright, Need they no created light;
Thou its light, its joy, its crown, Thou its sun which goes
not down;
There forever may we sing Alleluias to our King.

WHAT CHILD IS THIS

(In the hymn arrangement of this poem, the second half of
the first stanza constitutes a Refrain and only the first half
of stanzas 2 and 3 are used.)

What Child is this, who, laid to rest On Mary's lap is sleep-
ing?
Whom angels greet with anthems sweet, While shepherds
watch are keeping?
This, this is Christ the King, Whom shepherds guard and
angels sing:
Haste, haste to bring Him laud, the Babe, the Son of Mary!

Why lies He in such mean estate, Where ox and ass are
feeding?
Good Christian, fear: for sinners here The silent Word is
pleading.
Nails, spear, shall pierce Him through, The cross be borne,
for me, for you:
Hail, hail, the Word made flesh, The Babe, the Son of
Mary!

So bring Him incense, gold, and myrrh, Come, peasant,
King, to own Him:
The King of Kings salvation brings, Let loving hearts en-
throne Him.
Raise, raise the song on high, The Virgin sings her lullaby:
Joy, joy, for Christ is born, The Babe, the Son of Mary!

Chapter III

BRIGHTEST AND BEST OF THE SONS OF THE MORNING

BRIGHTEST AND BEST OF THE
SONS OF THE MORNING

A daughter's Christmas Eve request and another dutiful daughter's handy composition book played important roles in the creation of two of Christendom's finest Christmas hymns.

John Byrom (1692-1763), a contemporary and co-worker of Rev. John Wesley and his hymn-writing brother, Rev. Charles Wesley, asked one of his daughters, Dolly, on Christmas Eve, 1749, "What would you like for a Christmas present tomorrow morning, dear?" She replied in a most unorthodox fashion to her minister-physician-inventor father, "Please write me a poem." While writing an original poem would hardly be a difficult task for the man who gave to the English language the names "Tweedledum and Tweedledee," undoubtedly Byrom was surprised as well as shocked by the simplicity and sincerity of his daughter's request. "Not a dress or a doll, not a trinket or a toy, but the thing she knows I can give her which will have in it so much more of myself than anything else, a poem," the delighted father must have said to himself as he pondered her strange reply later that evening.

Byrom has been described as an extremely tall man who invariably carried a stick with a crooked top, and who always wore in public a "curious low-polled slouched hat, from under the long-peaked front brim of which his benignant face bent forward a cautiously inquisitive sort of look as if he were in the habit of prying into everything without caring to let everything enter deeply into him." It was this remarkable man who invented a new system of writing short hand, teaching it to such leading citizens of his day as the Wesley brothers, thus enabling Charles to write down many of his original hymns in short hand, before the flow of ideas stopped or his inspiration left him. Anyway, acceding to Dolly's desire, her father proceeded to do exactly what she had asked him to do, and the next morning, Christmas Day, she found a sheet of paper at her place at the breakfast table, on which he had written the six stanzas of his Christmas hymn, which began:

> *Christians, awake! salute the happy morn*
> *Whereon the Saviour of the world was born;*
> *Rise to adore the mystery of love,*
> *Which hosts of angels chanted from above;*
> *With them the joyful tidings first begun,*
> *Of God Incarnate and the Virgin's Son.*

In like manner, one of the noblest hymn-writers in the English language, Reginald Heber (1783-1826) wrote the greatest missionary hymn of the nineteenth century, exactly one hundred years after Isaac Watts had published the finest missionary hymn of the preceding century, "Jesus Shall Reign," in 1719. It was at the request of his father-in-law, Dean Shipley, of Wrexham Cathedral in North Wales, that thirty-six-year-old Heber, on the Friday afternoon before Pentecost (Whit Sunday), 1819, wrote the four stanzas of his magnificent hymn "From Greenland's Icy Mountains." The new hymn was read the following Sunday morning, Pentecost, 1819, and the original manuscript sold some years later for $210.00, an amount reputed to have been larger than the missionary offering the hymn had been written to inspire!

Heber, like Byrom before him, was no novice in the field of letters, having won the coveted Newdigate Prize for Poetry at Oxford University while a student of seventeen at Brasenose College in 1800. The reading of his remarkable four-hundred-line poem on "Palestine" received such applause as had never before been heard in that sedate gathering. In the majestic lines of this poem, Heber gave evidence of the florid, fluent and picturesque style which was to permeate the hymns he was to write during the years

of his active ministry, both as a curate in his
native England and later as Bishop of the Anglican Church in India. In the passage describing
the coming of the Messiah, Heber had written
these lines:

> *Nor vain their hope, bright-beaming from the sky*
> *Burst in full blaze the Day-Spring from on high;*
> *Earth's utmost isle exulted at the sight,*
> *And crowding nations drank the orient light.*
> *Lo, star-led chiefs Assyrian odours bring,*
> *And bending Magi seek their infant king!*
> *Messiah comes—let furious discord cease,*
> *Be peace on earth before the Prince of Peace!*

While working on this lengthy poetic history
of Palestine, Reginald and his brother, Richard,
served as personal guides for the great Scottish
poet and novelist, Sir Walter Scott, on a tour of
Oxford and Blenheim. Reginald read some of
these lines to the famous northern man of letters
at breakfast one morning at Brasenose College,
whereupon Scott suggested that the writer include some reference to the tools that were used
by Solomon's craftsmen in erecting the Temple
in Jerusalem. Acting immediately upon that ad-
vice, Heber added these lines to his poem:

> *No hammer fell, no ponderous axes rung;*
> *Like some tall palm the mystic fabric sprung.*

In 1807 when Heber had completed his education and taken Holy Orders, he began his min-

istry at Hodnet, a little village in western England, serving in the dual capacity of country squire and village vicar, positions he was to fill with sympathy and understanding for a period of sixteen years. It was in 1811, four years after assuming the responsibilities of the Hodnet parish, that Heber picked up a small composition book belonging to one of his daughters, and, in the neat and legible manner that characterized all of his manuscripts, wrote down the five stanzas of an Epiphany hymn.

The birth of Christ is celebrated on the twenty-fifth of December, the day soon enough after the winter solstice wherein the days begin to grow longer, thus appropriately commemorating the birthday anniversary of Him whom God sent to scatter the darkness of sin with the Light of Life. Since no one knows precisely when our Lord was born, this day was settled upon several centuries after the beginning of the Christian era as most fitting for celebrating the coming of the Son of God, of whom St. John had said in his Gospel, "The light shineth in the darkness and the darkness could not put it out" (John 1:5). Had Jesus been born in the dead of winter, when, as Christina Rossetti (1830-1894) said, in her beautiful Christmas hymn, "In The Bleak Mid-winter,"

> *Earth stood hard as iron, Water like a stone,*
> *Snow had fallen, snow on snow, Snow on snow,*

the shepherds would not have been out on the hills "keeping watch over their flocks by night" but would have had their sheep bedded down in the shelter and safety of a cave or shed. Nor would Joseph have taken Mary, being "great with child," on the perilous journey from Nazareth to Bethlehem "to be enrolled" at the order of the Roman Emperor, Augustus Caesar.

But the second Advent festival which radiates all the warmth and glow of Christmas comes twelve days later, on the sixth of January, and is known as Epiphany, which means literally "the showing-up" or "the appearing" of the wise men at the cradle of the new-born King. This later festival commemorates the appearing of the Magi, and its observation through the centuries has inspired such plays as Shakespeare's "Twelfth Night" and such festive songs as "The Twelve Days of Christmas" during which a lover was expected to bring his beloved a special gift for each of the twelve days, the recipient finally ending up with an odd assortment of presents including: twelve drummers drumming, eleven lords a-leaping, ten ladies waltzing, nine pipers piping, eight maids a-milking, seven swans a-swimming, six geese a-laying, five golden rings, four mocking birds, three French hens, two turtle doves and a partridge in a pear tree!

Anyway, these gala feast-days provided the

occasion for Heber's new hymn, and had not his daughter's notebook been handy, the chances are that the inspiration would have left him before he could have gone into his study, found a piece of paper, dipped his pen in the inkwell and written down the lines that were rushing into his mind in such prolific profusion. In his hymn the "Assyrian odours" of his prize poem became "the odours of Edom," while the "Messiah" who was to come was worshipped as "Maker and Monarch and Saviour of all." His florid style is seen in the flowing movement of his opening stanza, one he repeated at the close of his hymn, as the fifth and final stanza:

> *Brightest and best of the sons of the morning,*
> *Dawn on our darkness and lend us Thine aid;*
> *Star of the east, the horizon adorning,*
> *Guide where our infant Redeemer is laid.*

Little did the poet dream when he wrote of "earth's utmost isles" in 1800 that in 1819 he would write the greatest missionary hymn of his century or that in 1823 he would respond to the insistent call of his Church to go to India as the Bishop of Calcutta, there to die after three short years of crowded and unusual activity and remarkable accomplishment, during which he ordained the first native of India ever to enter the Christian ministry.

The year after his untimely death at forty-three, Heber's devoted wife, Amelia, Dean Shipley's daughter, gathered together his finest hymns and sacred poems, publishing them in 1827 under the title "Hymns Written And Adapted To The Weekly Service of the Church Year." From that collection, "Holy, Holy, Holy," "The Son Of God Goes Forth To War," "From Greenland's Icy Mountains," "Bread Of The World," and his Epiphany hymn found their way into the hymnals of Christendom and Heber helped usher in a new day in the hymnody of his Church. Giving Christ the adoration of his heart, and devoting the last years of his life to the down-trodden and depressed of his vast Asiatic parish, the preacher-poet lived out the prayer with which he closed his Christmas hymn:

> *Vainly we offer each ample oblation,*
> *Vainly with gifts would His favor secure;*
> *Richer by far is the heart's adoration,*
> *Dearer to God are the prayers of the poor.*

BRIGHTEST AND BEST OF THE SONS OF THE MORNING

Brightest and best of the sons of the morning,
Dawn on our darkness and lend us thine aid;
Star of the east, the horizon adorning,
Guide where our infant Redeemer is laid.

Cold on his cradle the dewdrops are shining,
Low lies his head with the beasts of the stall;
Angels adore him in slumber reclining,
Maker and Monarch and Saviour of all.

Say, shall we yield him, in costly devotion,
Odours of Edom and offerings divine;
Gems of the mountain and pearls of the ocean,
Myrrh from the forest and gold from the mine.

Vainly we offer each ample oblation,
Vainly with gifts would his favor secure;
Richer by far is the heart's adoration,
Dearer to God are the prayers of the poor.

Brightest and best of the sons of the morning,
Dawn on our darkness and lend us thine aid;
Star of the east, the horizon adorning,
Guide where our infant Redeemer is laid.

Chapter IV

HARK THE HERALD ANGELS SING

HARK THE HERALD ANGELS SING

The Rev. Charles Wesley wrote his first famous hymn on the day that he felt his heart strangely warmed, Pentecost (Whit Sunday), May 20, 1738, and his last hymn the day that he died, Saturday, March 29, 1788. During the fifty years in between he penned about sixty-five hundred more, making him the most prolific as well as the most profound hymn writer in the entire history of Christendom.

In his first hymn he took a rather pointed jab at his distinguished university professor brother, Rev. John Wesley, who had been told by their mother, Susanna, that he was a "brand plucked from the burning" after a dramatic last-minute rescue from the flaming parsonage at Epworth, England, where both of the boys had been born, and where their honored father, Rev. Samuel Wesley, served many years as pastor and preacher. Charles must have tired of hearing his older brother John relate this incident over and over again, but he bided his time until his thirty-first year, when he began his first hymn with these revealing lines:

Where shall my wondering soul begin?
How shall I all to heaven aspire?
A slave redeemed from death and sin,
A brand plucked from eternal fire.

In this way he notified his preacher brother that God had saved him for the ministry too, and that he felt he was as much a "plucked brand" as Susanna had said John was!

The very next year, when Charles was thirty-two, he wrote three of his noblest hymns. The first was written on the anniversary day of his "conversion" and contained about eighteen stanzas, several of which are embodied in the hymn that is loved by Methodists the world over, "O For A Thousand Tongues To Sing." The second became the finest Easter hymn in the English language, "Christ The Lord Is Risen Today," while the third constitutes Wesley's best contribution to the hymnody of Christmastide. Later, when the Advent poem of this "Anglican clergyman turned Methodist" was wedded to a tune composed by a Christianized Jewish musician, Christendom came into possession of one of its most glorious hymns celebrating the birth of Christ.

By the time Charles Wesley sat down to write his carol, he had already had more than his share of adventure and travel. He had visited the New World, travelling to the colony of Georgia in America as secretary to the colony's founder,

General Oglethorpe, while his brother John went primarily to convert the Indians. The trip turned out to be a tragic mistake as well as a comedy of errors, and Charles sailed for England just a few short months after arriving in America while John stuck it out for a couple more years before coming home as disillusioned and disgusted as his younger brother.

It could have been his association with the great pioneer hymn writer, Rev. Isaac Watts (1674-1748) that inspired Charles to bring to glorious fruition what the older clergyman had begun to do in the field of hymnody. But once kindled, the spark of genius burned to a full flame, ushering in an era rarely equalled and never surpassed in the history of the Christian Church.

It was while meditating upon the birth of Our Lord that Charles (who, while a student at Oxford University had founded the much-maligned "Holy Club" whose methodical activities had given birth to the word "Methodist" on the part of some sarcastic, ridiculing, worldly minded classmates) sat down and wrote the first of ten four-line stanzas that contained these words:

Hark! how all the welkin rings, "Glory to the King of Kings,
Peace on earth and mercy mild, God and sinners reconciled."

Along with many others, this hymn was published the year of its composition in a Wesleyan volume entitled simply "Hymns And Sacred Poems." In subsequent hymnals, Wesley's ten stanzas underwent a series of alterations and adjustments until the Rev. George Whitefield, a co-worker in the Wesleyan revival and one of the most impressive preachers of his century, settled the matter once and for all by eliminating the rather awkward word "welkin" (an old English word for "the vault of heaven") and substituting a new phrase which read:

Hark! the herald angels sing, "Glory to the new-born King."

In that manner Whitefield published the hymn in his "Collection" of 1753, and it is in this form that the stanzas have survived. The composer Felix Mendelssohn (1809-1847) was born a Jew, but when his father, Abraham, became a convert to the Christian religion, the name "Bartholdy" had been added to the noble family name. Mendelssohn in his century became almost as prolific a composer as Charles Wesley was a poet, and had he lived as long as the Methodist pioneer doubtless would have equalled his creative output in his chosen field. When a celebration commemorating Gutenberg's invention of the printing press was planned, Mendelssohn was commissioned to compose suitable music for the anniversary, as a result of which he composed his "Festgesang #7" in 1840, his thirty-first year.

Commenting upon his music, the gifted German said, "I am sure that piece will be liked very much by singers and hearers but it will never do to sacred words." An English Doctor of Music, William H. Cummings (1831-1915), proved the master wrong, when, in 1855, he suddenly discovered that the second chorus of Mendelssohn's music was perfect for Wesley's words, provided two four-line stanzas were combined to make one eight-line stanza, with the first two lines of the opening stanza being repeated as a "Chorus" or "Refrain." Since its publication in 1856, it has supplanted every other tune to which the stanzas had formerly been sung, and now is generally recognized as one of the most inspiring tunes the composer was privileged to write during his brief life of thirty-eight years. Although Mendelssohn considered his tune a "secular" one, the unanimous verdict of Christians the world over assures it a permanent place in their hymnody as a "sacred" piece, ranking with the loftiest passages from his oratorio "Elijah."

While the composer would be surprised if he were to know of the adaptation of his music and its subsequent popularity in the intervening years, the poet would be shocked if he were to read some of the "watered down" versions of several of his noble lines. For, in order not to ruffle the delicate and refined (?) spiritual sensitivities of some ultra-liberals who see no reason for believing in or accepting the Virgin Birth of Jesus, editors have taken the sharp edge off of Wesley's words and dulled his poignant lines,

"Late in time behold Him come, Offspring of the Virgin's womb,"

to read,

"Long desired behold Him come, Finding here His humble home"

or

"To the earth from heaven's home."

Be that as it may, of all the more than six thousand majestic hymns that flowed "like a perennial flood" from Wesley's pen during his half-century of creative endeavour, this hymn alone was deemed worthy of a place in the Anglican "Book of Common Prayer." By-passing such Wesleyan favorites as "Jesus, Lover Of My Soul," "Love Divine," "Come, O Thou Traveller Unknown" which Isaac Watts claimed was Wesley's greatest, and even "A Charge To Keep I Have," the committee of the Established Church agreed to include only "Hark, The Herald Angels Sing." Some scholars claim that Charles was ignored because the Wesleys were out of favor with the Church of England following the organization of the Methodist Church, while others are of the opinion that the committee needed a full page hymn for the last page in the book and that this particular one filled the bill. Still others are confident that in this way the Anglican communion paid its restrained respects to the Wesleys but in a manner that would keep them silent eleven months out of every year, since "Hark, The Herald Angels Sing" is used only in December, at the Advent season.

Anyway, a more joyous Christmas hymn would be difficult to discover and this carol, which resulted from the combined genius of Wesley, Whitefield, Mendelssohn and Cummings enters its second century of usefulness in higher favor than ever before. Undoubtedly, Christians will be singing it for as many Christmases in the future as there have been since the time of the birth of Jesus and the writing of the original stanzas in 1739.

"Come, Thou Long Expected Jesus," Wesley's second-best Christmas hymn, was not written until five years later, in 1744. Due to poor musical settings, it suffered unmerited obscurity until matched with the stirring strains of the hymn tune "Hyfrydol," one of Rowland H. Prichard's (1811-1887) best compositions, dated 1855. Since that fortunate wedding of words and music, the hymn has rapidly gained favor and is growing in popularity and use with the passing of the years. The fact that two of Wesley's Christmas hymns are in common usage today is a tribute to his glowing heart as well as to his poetic genius.

Hark the Herald Angels Sing

*Hark, the herald angels sing, "Glory to the new-born
    King;*
*Peace on earth and mercy mild; God and sinners recon-
    ciled."*
Joyful all ye nations rise, Join the triumphs of the skies;
*With the angelic hosts proclaim, "Christ is born in Bethle-
    hem."*

*Christ, by highest heaven adored, Christ, the everlasting
    Lord;*
*Late in time behold him come, Offspring of the virgin's
    womb.*
Veiled in flesh the Godhead see, Hail the incarnate Deity!
Pleased as man with men to dwell, Jesus, our Immanuel.

*Hail, the heaven-born Prince of Peace! Hail the Sun of
    righteousness!*
*Light and life to all he brings, Risen with healing in his
    wings;*
Mild he lays his glory by, Born that man no more may die;
*Born to raise the sons of earth, Born to give them second
    birth.*

Come, Desire of nations, come! Fix in us thy humble home;
*Rise, the woman's conquering Seed, Bruise in us the ser-
    pent's head.*

Adam's likeness now efface, Stamp thine image in its place;
Second Adam from above, Reinstate us in thy love.
> *Hark, the herald angels sing, "Glory to the new-*
> *born King."*

COME, THOU LONG EXPECTED JESUS

Come, Thou long expected Jesus! Born to set thy people
> *free;*
From our fears and sins release us, Let us find our rest in
> *thee:*
Israel's strength and consolation, Hope of all the saints thou
> *art;*
Dear Desire of every nation — Joy of every longing heart.

Born, thy people to deliver; Born a child, and yet a king;
Born to reign in us forever, Now thy gracious kingdom
> *bring.*
By thine own eternal Spirit, Rule in all our hearts alone:
By thine all-sufficient merit, Raise us to thy glorious throne.

Chapter V

IT CAME UPON
THE MIDNIGHT CLEAR

IT CAME UPON
THE MIDNIGHT CLEAR

Father Joseph Mohr who wrote the stanzas of "Silent Night" was a Roman Catholic priest, while Phillips Brooks, the Bostonian of "O Little Town of Bethlehem" fame was a renowned Episcopalian preacher and Bishop. Rev. Isaac Watts, who fathered "Joy To The World" was a clergyman of the Church of England, the Anglican Church, as was Rev. Reginald Heber, who penned "Brightest And Best Of The Sons Of The Morning." Rev. Charles Wesley, an Anglican clergyman turned Methodist, gave us "Hark, The Herald Angels Sing" while an American Episcopalian, Rev. John H. Hopkins, Jr., wrote both words and music of "We Three Kings Of Orient Are." James Montgomery, the Sheffield, England, newspaperman, and author of "Hail To The Lord's Anointed," and "Angels From The Realms Of Glory" belonged to the Moravians. The only Unitarian clergyman who produced a Christmas hymn that outlived his own day and generation was a New Englander, Rev. Edmund Hamilton Sears (1810-1876). Other Unitarians have written hymns that have been accepted by the Church at large, among them Mrs. Sarah Flower Adams, the talented Englishwoman whose hymn "Nearer My God To Thee" is a universal favorite, and the Americans, Oliver Wendell Holmes, Rev. Samuel Longfellow (Henry Wadsworth's younger brother) and Rev. Frederick L. Hosmer, all three of whom wrote hymns that are found in the hymnals of major denominations today. When the theological controversies between orthodox Trinitarians and extreme Unitarians were raging throughout Christendom, the hymns of the Unitarians were barred from the hymnals of Evangelical Trinitarian Churches. While one strictly conservative Trinitarian is supposed to have said, when "Nearer My God To Thee" was first proposed for an American hymnal, "The hymn by that English Unitarian will go in this book over my dead body!" it would be almost over the dead bodies of today's editorial committees that it would be left out! The lines of demarcation that once separated the two opposing groups have grown less distinct with the passing of time.

Even though the author of "It Came Upon The Midnight Clear" was proud of his connection with the Unitarian fellowship, he had no reservations about believing and preaching from his New England pulpits the divinity of Jesus Christ. That can be understood only as one differentiates between the words "deity" and "divinity." The Unitarians reject the deity of Christ, which means they do not believe that Jesus Christ was equal with God. But they do accept his divinity, the teaching that Jesus was inferior to God but superior to man. They claim Jesus was divine just as all of God's children are divine, rejecting the doctrine of the Holy Trinity (God for us as Father, God with us as Son, God in us as Holy Spirit) as un-Scriptural and therefore unnecessary.

The emotional excesses of early revivalists who claimed to be "filled with the Spirit" led many intellectual Christians to deny the existence of such a Holy Spirit, and, in their search for a satisfactory faith, to settle upon these cardinal points: the oneness of God, the humanity of Jesus, the perfectibility of human character, the natural character of the Bible and the ultimate salvation of every soul. To this group, that counted many of its most devoted adherents among the leaders in the college and university life of New England, Rev. Mr. Sears gave his own personal allegiance.

Having sprung from the loins of the Congregational Church, Unitarians included liberal Congregationalists in addition to Episcopalians in their following, and some of their leaders proved to be more evangelical than the basic tenets of the Church's creed allowed.

Sears completed his preparation for the ministry at Harvard Divinity School, graduating in 1837. Two years later he was ordained to the Christian ministry in the Unitarian Church in Wayland, Massachusetts. Instead of gazing with envious eyes at the large metropolitan pulpits in the growing cities of the north, Sears "had no other ambition than to lead such a quiet pastorate as Goldsmith described in his famous poem 'The Deserted Village.'" This he did in four pastorates, two at Wayland, separated only by a brief ministry in Lancaster in the same state, and a period of recuperation at a small farm near Wayland following a physical breakdown at Lancaster, brought on by overwork. His last ten years were spent serving the Unitarians at Weston, Massachusetts, where he died in January, 1876. While he never considered himself a poet of unusual skill or even a better-than-average hymn writer, Sears walks in the company of those select few who have had more than one Christmas hymn accepted by the Church. In that number are included such men of talent as Charles Wesley, James Montgomery and William C. Dix.

There is a remarkable similarity between Sears' two carols, although his first was penned in 1834, when the preacher was twenty-four, and the second was written fifteen years later, in 1849, when he was a mature minister of thirty-nine. Both were written in the same poetic meter, familiarly known as Common Meter Doubled (C.M.D.), each stanza having eight lines, with the first, third, fifth and seventh lines having eight syllables each, while the second, fourth, sixth and eighth had six syllables each. In fact, the stanzas of his first carol, "Calm On The Listening Ear Of Night," could have been part of his second carol, "It Came Upon The Midnight Clear," so closely do they resemble each other in theme, content, phraseology, figures of speech and conclusion. The first carol appeared in print in 1834, in the columns of the *Boston Observer* and gave early evidence of the skill and soul of the author. The opening stanza contained these lilting lines, which inspired so learned a man as Oliver Wendell Holmes to praise it as "one of the finest and most beautiful ever written,"

Calm on the listening ear of night Come heaven's melodious strains,
Where wild Judaea stretches far Her silver-mantled plains.
Celestial choirs, from courts above, Shed sacred glories there,
And angels, with their sparkling lyres, Make music on the air.

(This hymn can be sung to the same tune "Carol" to which "It Came Upon The Midnight Clear" is universally sung. The music was adapted from a musical study of composer-editor Richard S.

Willis (1819-1900) by Uzziah C. Burnap in 1850, when Sears' second Advent hymn was published for the first time.) The preacher's longing for universal peace and his consciousness that its realization was only a dream apart from the coming of Christ, led him to include in both of his hymns the same emphasis on the promise of the angels that first Christmas, "Peace on earth, goodwill to men." His first carol closed with these moving words:

"Glory to God!" the lofty strain The realms of ether fills;
  How sweeps the song of solemn joy O'er Judah's sacred hills!
"Glory to God!" the sounding skies Loud with their anthems ring;
"Peace on the earth, good-will to men, From heaven's eternal King."

Fifteen years later, "heaven's eternal King" became "heaven's all-gracious King," while the "calm" night became a "clear" one, as the "song of solemn joy" of 1834 was supplanted by a world that lay in "solemn stillness" in 1849. Compare the last stanza of his first carol with the first stanza of his last carol:

It came upon the midnight clear, That glorious song of old,
From angels bending near the earth To touch their harps of gold;
"Peace on the earth, good will to men, From heaven's all-gracious King."
The world in solemn stillness lay To hear the angels sing.

In both hymns the pastor plead with all men to hearken to the song of the angels, begging them in 1834 to "catch the anthem that from heaven rolled!" with its

"high and solemn lay— Glory to God! on earth be peace;
Salvation comes today"

and reminding them again in 1849 to

"hush the noise, ye men of strife, And hear the angels
sing!"

He had faith to foresee "the age of gold" of which the prophets had sung in bygone days, and he pictured it as the time when the whole world would send back to heaven the angelic song of peace "which now the angels sing."

Sears was privileged to write many books during his "quiet pastorates" in Massachusetts, bringing him such well-deserved fame that his Alma Mater honored him with a Doctor of Divinity degree in 1871. Two years later he was invited to preach in several Churches in England, a trip he thoroughly enjoyed, for large congregations attended his preaching, having known of him in advance by his books and his hymns. Few Americans have been more signally honored than this humble Unitarian pastor, for the Church at large has accepted two of his Christmas hymns, considering them among the finest in the English language. And undoubtedly they will continue to be sung until the vision of peace which haunts every true Christian heart becomes a reality, individually and collectively.

It Came Upon the Midnight Clear

It came upon the midnight clear, That glorious song of old,
From angels bending near the earth To touch their harps of gold;
"Peace on the earth, good will to men, From heaven's all-gracious King."
The world in solemn stillness lay To hear the angels sing.

Still through the cloven skies they come With peaceful wings unfurled,
And still their heavenly music floats O'er all the weary world;
Above its sad and lowly plains They bend on hovering wing,
And ever o'er its Babel sounds The blessed angels sing.

Yet with the woes of sin and strife The world has suffered long;
Beneath the heavenly strain have rolled Two-thousand years of wrong;
And man, at war with man, hears not The tidings which they bring;
O hush the noise, ye men of strife, And hear the angels sing.

O ye, beneath life's crushing load, Whose forms are bending low,
Who toil along the climbing way With painful steps and slow,

Look now! for glad and golden hours Come swiftly on the
 wing;
O rest beside the weary road And hear the angels sing!

For lo! the days are hastening on, By prophet bards
 foretold,
When with the ever-circling years Comes round the age of
 gold;
When peace shall over all the earth Its ancient splendors
 fling,
And the whole world send back the song Which now the
 angels sing.

Calm on the Listening Ear of Night

Calm on the listening ear of night Come heaven's melodious
 strains,
Where wild Judaea stretches far Her silver-mantled plains.
Celestial choirs from courts above Shed sacred glories
 there;
And angels, with their sparkling lyres, Make music on the
 air.

The answering hills of Palestine Send back the glad reply,
And greet, from all their holy heights, The Day-spring
 from on high.
O'er the blue depths of Galilee There comes a holier calm,
And Sharon waves, in solemn praise, Her silent groves of
 palm.

"Glory to God!" the sounding skies Loud with their
 anthems ring,
"Peace to the earth, good will to men, From heaven's
 eternal King!"
Light on thy hills, Jerusalem! The Saviour now is born;
More bright on Bethlehem's joyous plains Breaks the first
 Christmas morn.

Chapter VI

JOY TO THE WORLD

JOY TO THE WORLD

Isaac Watts wrote his first poem when he was seven and his last when he was in his seventies, and in between he gave Christendom some of the noblest and most sublime hymns in the English language. His initial offering was far from a hymn, but it won a prize of a farthing which Mrs. Watts had promised the child who wrote the best poem in a family contest. Young Isaac, the eldest of nine children, won with this couplet:

I write not for a farthing, but to try
How I your farthing authors can outvie!

Eleven years later, Watts (1674-1748) a native of Southampton, England, produced his first hymn, as much to protest against the cheap doggerel currently in use in services of public worship as to give expression to his own developing religious convictions. Rebelling against such trashy verses as:

'Tis like the precious ointment Down Aaron's beard did
*   flow,*
Down Aaron's beard it downward went, His garment
*   skirts unto;*

the eighteen-year-old son of stern-visaged Deacon Watts dared to criticize and complain only to hear his father reply with the well-worn argument of all elders to upstart youths, "Those hymns were good enough for your grandfather and your father, son, so they will have to be good enough for you." Undaunted, Isaac, encouraged by his brother Enoch, came back with this statement, "They will never do for me, father, regardless of what you and your father thought of them." Then the angry senior Mr. Watts shouted, "If you don't like the hymns we sing, then write better ones!" to which the brilliant youth replied, "I have written better ones, father, and if you will relax and listen, I will read one for you." When his father finally quieted down, the lad picked up a piece of paper and read aloud his first hymn, based upon Revelation 5:6-10:

Behold the glories of the Lamb, Amidst His Father's
    throne;
Prepare new honors for His Name, And Songs as yet un-
    known.

The amazed Deacon took a copy of his son's hymn to Church the following Sunday morning where it was "lined out" to the congregation. It was so well received that young Isaac was requested to prepare another new hymn for the next Sunday and then another for the next, a continuing request he filled for two hundred and twenty-two consecutive Sundays, single-handedly revolutionizing the congregational singing habits of the English Churches.

Very early in his life, Isaac had learned the Psalms of the Church, not only in services of public worship but also from his parents in their home. When Father Watts was imprisoned for his religious views on one occasion, Mother Watts carried young Isaac in her arms to the prison gate, where she on the outside and he on the inside sang together the metrical versions of the Psalms which comprised their hymnal. Preparing himself for the Christian ministry, Isaac took Holy Orders, preaching his first public sermon as an Anglican minister on his twenty-first birthday, from the pulpit of the Independent Church in London's Mark Lane.

In 1705 Watts published his first volume of original hymns and sacred poems, following it with "Hymns and Spiritual Songs" two years later, in 1707, a volume famous because it contained such majestic masterpieces as "Alas And Did My Saviour Bleed" and "When I Survey The Wondrous Cross."

One of the readers of this book, Miss Elizabeth Singer, felt that in Isaac Watts, whom she knew only through his published writings, she had finally found her true soul-mate, and a meeting between the two was arranged. When they met, she gazed in amazement at a little man "only five feet tall, with a sallow face, hooked nose, prominent cheek bones, small eyes and deathlike color" and promptly refused his proposal of marriage. That was as close as Watts ever came to committing matrimony! Some years later the lady confessed to a friend, "I admired the jewel but not the casket." It could have been soon after this unfortunate affair that Watts wrote:

*How vain are all things here below, How false and yet so
    fair!*

In 1712, declining health compelled Watts to resign his pulpit, an act in which the congregation concurred with great reluctance, and the preacher-poet accepted an invitation from the Lord Mayor of London, Sir Thomas, and Lady Abney, to recuperate at their spacious estate. Going with the intention of staying only a few weeks, Watts remained as the guest of the Abneys for thirty-six years. Sir Thomas made Watts the private Chaplain of his household, while his wife said of their distinguished visitor's lengthy stay, "It was the shortest visit a friend ever paid a friend."

During his stay at the Abneys, Watts devoted himself to the completion of a project that had long been on his heart, the preparation of a volume of hymns based upon the Psalms of David, in which he planned to Christianize the

Psalms by reading back into them all of the glow and glory of the New Testament story. In 1715 his collection of hymns and poems for children came from the press, but not until 1719 was his monumental work, "The Psalms of David, Imitated," ready for publication. In preparing this volume, Watts read back into the Ninety-eighth Psalm all of the joy of the coming of the Messiah. Basing his hymn principally on verses 4 (Make a joyful noise unto the Lord, all the earth; make a loud noise and rejoice and sing praise), 6 (Make a joyful noise before the Lord), 8 and 9 (Let the floods clap their hands, let the hills be joyful together before the Lord, for he cometh to judge the earth, with righteousness shall he judge the world), he wrote his finest Christmas hymn, beginning with these lines:

Joy to the world, The Lord is come, Let earth receive her King;
Let every heart prepare Him room, And heav'n and nature sing.

Later Rev. Charles Wesley, taking his cue from Dr. Watts, read back into the Levitical account of the Jewish Year of Jubilee all of the glory of salvation and redemption in Christ Jesus, and penned his hymn "Blow Ye The Trumpet, Blow!" In this same volume, the poet-preacher included his poetic version of Psalm

Ninety (Lord, thou hast been our dwelling place in all generations), "O God, Our Help In Ages Past" and his rendition of Psalm Seventy-Two (verse 6: He shall have dominion also from sea to sea)," "Jesus Shall Reign, Where'er The Sun," the first missionary hymn in the English language.

Seventy years after the publication of this magnificent book, there were still some Christians who believed that God stopped singing when David died, and for believers to sing anything other than the metrical versions of the Old Testament Psalms was heresy of the worst sort. They despised the hymns of Watts and Wesley because they were "of human composition," while accepting the crudest versifications of the Psalms by their own contemporaries on the ground that they rendered the words of the Bible poetically in the English tongue and in a suitable meter so they could be sung to accepted tunes. In fact, when the first General Assembly of the Presbyterian Church in the United States convened in the Second Presbyterian Church in Philadelphia in May, 1789, Rev. Adam Rankin rode horseback from his Kentucky parish to the seat of the Assembly to plead with his fellow Presbyterians "to refuse to allow the great and pernicious error of adopting the use of Watts' hymns in public worship in preference to Rouse's versifications of the Psalms of David." The Assembly heard him patiently, and then, with Calvinistic wisdom, requested him to exercise Christian charity toward those who differed from him in their views, and to guard against disturbing the peace of the Church on this matter!

Strangely enough, nine years earlier, in May, 1780, during the American Revolutionary War, a detachment of British forces had sallied forth from their Staten Island headquarters and burned the nearby town of Elizabeth, New Jersey, in what became known as "The Battle of Springfield." Among the casualties was the wife of the local Presbyterian pastor, Rev. James Caldwell. When the enemy attempted a repeat performance three weeks later, George Washington's militia was on the ground, all lined up to give battle. Suddenly the defenders discovered that there was a tragic shortage of wadding for their guns. When Rev. Mr. Caldwell heard the news, he rushed back to his Church, picked up an armful of hymnals, and hurried to the scene of the impending battle. Handing the hymnals to the fighters up and down the line, he cried out, "Give 'em Watts, boys; Give 'em Watts!" The desperate soldiers tore out the pages of the hymnals, wadded their guns and gave the enemy what the Chaplain had commanded!

Since that day, many an individual battle has been won as Christians have taken up the great hymns of the faith and given the devil Watts when sorely pressed by the evil one, and the Sword of the Spirit, which is the Word of God, in poetry as well as in prose, has never failed to destroy the enemy!

Set to a musical theme adapted by Dr. Lowell Mason (1792-1872) from "The Messiah" by George Frederick Handel (1685-1759), "Joy To The World" is, as its first word suggests, one of the most joyous hymns of the Christmas season.

The bachelor poet also wrote the lovely cradle song, "Hush, My Dear, Lie Still And Slumber, Holy Angels Guard Thy Bed," which children the world over sing at Christmas time, since a more beautiful description of the birth of Jesus in poetic form for little children would be difficult to discover.

JOY TO THE WORLD

Joy to the world! the Lord is come!
Let earth receive her King.
Let every heart prepare him room,
And heav'n and nature sing.

Joy to the earth! the Saviour reigns;
Let men their songs employ;
While fields and floods, rocks, hills and plains,
Repeat the sounding joy.

No more let sins and sorrows grow,
Nor thorns infest the ground;
He comes to make his blessings flow
Far as the curse is found.

He rules the world with truth and grace;
And makes the nations prove
The glories of his righteousness,
And wonders of his love.

CRADLE SONG

Dr. Watts' original song contained seven eight-line stanzas. This version consists of the first complete stanza and the second half of stanza two coupled with the first half of stanza six. These lines may be sung to John Wyeth's tune "Nettleton," to which tune "Come Thou Fount Of Every Blessing" is now universally sung.

Hush, my dear, lie still and slumber,
    holy angels guard thy bed;
Heavenly blessings without number
    gently falling on thy head.
Sleep my babe, thy food and raiment,
    house and home thy friends provide,
All without thy care or payment,
    all thy wants are well supplied.

Soft and easy is thy cradle,
    coarse and hard thy Saviour lay,
When his birth-place was a stable,
    and his softest bed was hay.
Lo! he slumbers in his manger,
    where the hornéd oxen fed;
Peace my darling, here's no danger,
    here's no Ox a-near thy bed.

Chapter VII

O COME, ALL YE FAITHFUL

O COME, ALL YE FAITHFUL

Astronomically or astronautically, "O Come, All Ye Faithful" could be called "The Gemini Hymn." Although Castor and Pollux do not appear by name, there are several "twins," "pairs" or "two-somes" involved in the hymn's fascinating history: two music copyists, two translations of the same Latin poem by the same British clergyman, and two magnificent sets of stanzas wedded to the same majestic tune, one set of which became the favorite hymn of two American Presidents.

The first music copyist was an Englishman, John Francis Wade (1710-1786), from Lancashire, who spent most of his adult and creative years in exile at Douay (Douai), France. In this French Roman Catholic community there was an English college which became a haven of refuge for many British exiles during the Jacobite rebellion of 1745. Jacobites were "loyal adherents of the British Catholic monarch, James II, or his direct descendants, after the English Revolution of 1688." Wade copied music manuscripts and made his living selling these copies to Catholics and Protestants in and around Douay, in addition to giving music lessons to a few apt pupils from the families of the more well-to-do residents of the community. While the eight stanzas of the Latin version of this Advent paean of praise have been attributed to many different poets, from the Roman Catholic Saint Bonaventura, to an anonymous monk of the Cistercian Order, it is now generally agreed that Mr. Wade either came across them or created them in connection with his music copying and research in Douay. As reliable an historian as Will Durant states that "Adeste Fidelis" was originally written by an unknown French poet between the years 1685 and 1690, during the reign of Louis XIV, although most hymnologists still credit them to the copyist himself. The eight Latin stanzas first appeared in print in John Wade's book, "Cantus Diversi," published in 1751, a copy of which has been preserved in the library of Stonyhurst College, Lancashire, England. The Obituary List in the Catholic Directory of 1787 makes this mention of the copyist-poet: "1786, August 16th, Mr. John Francis Wade, a layman, aged 75, with whose beautiful manuscript books our chapels as well as private families abound, in writing which and teaching the Latin and Church song he chiefly spent his time."

The French Revolution brought about the

demise of the Douay Colony not many years after Wade's death. Interestingly enough, Jesuit priests from England later brought "Adeste Fidelis" with them when they crossed the English Channel to France after the Revolution, completing the circle which had begun in Douay several decades earlier.

The second copyist was another Englishman, Samuel Webbe, Sr. (1740-1816). While Samuel and his mother were visiting relatives in England, the lad's father died on the Mediterranean island of Minorca, where he had filled a government position for many years. His death left his wife and heir destitute. Growing up in abject poverty, Samuel spent seven years apprenticed to a cabinet maker before deciding to dedicate his life to music. In order to finance his musical education he became a skilled music copyist, working so laboriously on some occasions that he remained at his writing desk from five o'clock in the morning until midnight. But he mastered music as well as several languages, and lived to become not only a well-known organist but also a talented composer. The first published appearance of the tune to which "O Come, All Ye Faithful" was to be forever associated was in Samuel Webbe's book, "Essay On Church Plain Chant," published in London in 1782. So the two music copyists, Wade and Webbe, were instrumental in giving Christendom her first glimpse of the words and music of one of her noblest Christmas hymns, "Adeste Fidelis."

One of those who was impressed by the published Latin version of this splendid poem was a British Anglican divine, Rev. Frederick Oakeley (1802-1880). An Oxford graduate, Oakeley took Holy Orders and was ordained a clergyman of the Church of England in 1826. After serving two appointments, he accepted the pulpit of the Margaret Street Chapel in London in 1839. He was so pleased with the eight stanzas that Wade had either discovered or created that, in 1841, he rendered them into his native English with a translation that began "Ye Faithful, Approach Ye." This new hymn was sung in Margaret Street Chapel to the tune which Samuel Webbe, Sr. had first published in 1782. While the new hymn became popular among the people of Oakeley's own parish, it never gained any wider recognition. Preacher-translator-poet Oakeley meanwhile underwent quite a profound change in his religious views, and, after publishing some pamphlets that were decidedly pro-Roman, he was suspended from his Protestant pulpit, and became a priest of the Roman Catholic communion in 1845. In this change he was following the example of a fellow-Anglican clergyman, Rev. John Henry Newman, of "Lead Kindly Light" fame, who also abandoned Protestantism for Catholicism that very same year. While hymn writer Newman eventually became a Cardinal, hymn-translator Oakeley became only a Canon.

Eleven years after translating, "Ye Faithful, Approach Ye," and seven years after forsaking the Church of England, Frederick Oakeley determined to improve upon his hymn. He studied the Latin more carefully in an attempt to translate it into more effective and impressive English, and repeated over and over again the words and phrases with which John Wade had immortalized himself in France:

> *Adeste fidelis, Laeti triumphantes;*
> *Venite, venite in Bethlehem.*
> *Natum videte, Regem Angelorum:*
> *Venite adoremus Dominum.*

The first, seventh and eighth stanzas of Wade's publication seemed to translator Oakeley to have more hymnic possibilities than any of the other stanzas. Soon he found himself translating them into forceful English, with the opening line of the first stanza, altered and improved, reading, "O Come, All Ye Faithful, Joyful And Triumphant." Whether the priest-poet's membership in the Roman communion had improved his understanding of Latin in the intervening years has never been determined!

Thus did a "Francisized Englishman" in collaboration with a "Catholicized Anglican" give to Christendom this majestic hymn that today is considered neither French nor English, and neither Catholic nor Protestant. It is about as ecumenical a Christmas hymn as exists in all hymnody.

Since Samuel Webbe, Sr. played the organ in the Chapel of the Portuguese Embassy in London and used this superb tune on many occasions, the music became known as "The Portuguese Hymn," leading some students to believe that it had its origin in Portugal. Scholars, however, knew better and never ceased to boast of its British origin. "O Come, All Ye Faithful" in its present poetic and musical form first appeared in F. H. Murray's collection, "A Hymnal For Use In The English Church," published in London in 1852. Sometimes, Protestants have a tendency to say that Martin Luther's hymn "A Mighty Fortress Is Our God" "belongs to us," just as some Catholics state that John Wade's "Adeste Fidelis" "belongs to us." The truth of the matter is that both hymns belong to all Christians, whether they swear fealty to a Roman Pontiff, a British Monarch or an American President.

The third of these "twins" or "pairs" consists in the fact that two of the stateliest hymns in the English language, "O Come, All Ye Faithful" and "How Firm A Foundation," are now sung to the same tune, "Adeste Fidelis" or "Portuguese Hymn." While the former came in Latin guise through an Englishman residing in France, the latter is credited to a poet known only by the single initial "K." Historians and hymnologists are agreed that "K" could be Robert Keene, who served as one of the Musical Directors of London's Carter Lane Baptist Church, during the distinguished sixty-three-year pastorate (1773-1836) of Rev. Dr. John Rippon. It was in the 1787 edition of Rippon's "Selection" ("A Selection of Hymns from the Best Authors, Intended as an Appendix to Dr. Watts' Psalms And Hymns") that "How Firm A Foundation" first appeared in print. The hymn proved so immediately and immensely popular that within three years it was included in an Anglican hymnal in Great Britain, as well as in a Baptist hymnal in the United States.

Significantly, "How Firm A Foundation" was the favorite hymn of two American Presidents: Andrew Jackson and Theodore Roosevelt. It was also the personal choice of General Robert E. Lee, who requested that it be sung at his funeral "as an expression of his full trust in the ways of the Heavenly Father."

Of the dozens of English translations of "Adeste Fidelis," Oakeley's still stands apart as a perfect example of poetic excellence. Its widespread popularity is well deserved, for a more harmonious blending of words and music, and a more appropriate and majestic Advent processional hymn does not exist in all of Christendom's Christmas hymnody.

O Come, All Ye Faithful

O come, all ye faithful, Joyful and triumphant,
O come ye, O come ye to Bethlehem.
Come and behold him, born the king of angels;
O come let us adore him, Christ the Lord.

Sing, choirs of angels, sing in exultation,
Sing, all ye citizens of heaven above.
Glory to God, all glory in the highest.
O come let us adore him, Christ the Lord.

Yea, Lord, we greet thee, born this happy morning,
Jesus, to thee be all glory given.
Word of the Father, now in flesh appearing;
O come let us adore him, Christ the Lord.

Chapter VIII

O LITTLE TOWN OF BETHLEHEM

O LITTLE TOWN OF BETHLEHEM

Although not a professional poet, Phillips Brooks could write a hymn, a carol or a poem with almost effortless ease. Rarely has any Protestant preacher caught the imagination of the intellectual and humble people of his day as did this large, robust, giant of a man and prince of the pulpit. Boston-born and Harvard-bred, Phillips Brooks (1835-1893) had the added advantage of a home in which a well-trained mind and a warm heart were equally evident and in which both could be cultivated for the glory of God. But life proved to be no bed of roses for the attractive and talented youth. In first public position as a Latin professor in one of his Alma Maters, the Boston Latin School, he was a miserable failure, a tragedy which led him to make this confession, "I have failed most signally in teaching school." It was only when he surrendered himself wholly and completely to the Christian ministry that he "came to himself" and his personal development and expanding usefulness in the years that followed vindicated the wisdom of his choice.

Entering the Episcopal Theological Seminary

at Alexandria, Virginia, he completed his "days of preparation" after which he was ordained in 1859, a young man of twenty-four, taking charge of a Church in the city of Philadelphia, where he was to remain for nearly ten years. It was there that he developed and mastered a pulpit style that was to lead him to the forefront among the pulpiteers of his generation. He felt he always had so much to say and so little time in which to say it that he cultivated a rapid-fire delivery that enabled him to deliver in thirty-five or forty minutes a sermon that would take the average minister at least an hour to proclaim. But the crowds hung upon his words and sought him out for personal counselling, a tribute to his loving and compassionate heart as well as to his brilliant and disciplined mind.

It was in 1865, while Brooks was serving the Holy Trinity Church in the City of Brotherly Love, that he planned a trip to the Holy Land. While his own congregation was so devoted to him as preacher and pastor that they were loath to give him up even for such an eventful trip, the people of the city urged him to go, one Church paper declaring "He will go accompanied with the prayers of thousands for his happy journeying and his safe return." The experience was all the thirty-year old bachelor dreamed it would be and Christmas week found him with his travelling party in Jerusalem, the

Holy City. On December 24, Christmas Eve, he
made the trip from Jerusalem to Bethlehem, the
City of David, on horseback, later writing in his
diary this interesting account, "Before dark we
rode out of town to the field where they say the
shepherds saw the star. It is a fenced piece of
ground with a cave in it, in which, strangely
enough, they put the shepherds." Later that
same night he attended the traditional services
in an ancient basilica said to have been built by
the Emperor Constantine early in the fourth
century, The Church of the Nativity. The five
hour service, from ten at night until three o'clock
Christmas morning, made an unforgettable im-
pression upon the youthful clergyman. When
he returned to America he still had "Palestine
singing in his soul," but the song he was eventually to sing as a result of his travels was almost
three years away.

As the popular minister prepared his Christmas program and services for December, 1868, he
did not realize that it would be his last and most
significant Christmas in Philadelphia, for the
following year brought with it the invitation to
Boston and the pulpit of historic Trinity Church.
Pondering over his Christmas services that year,
Brooks thought again of his visit to the Holy
Land three years earlier and the impressions and
inspiration that seemed to be indelibly stamped
upon his heart. When preparation was thus

combined with memory and the forward look with the backward glance, the pastor-poet was moved to express his feelings and sentiments in a lovely poem, written especially with the children of his parish in mind. With the soul of a true seer, he captured the mystery of that first Christmas in a carol which began with these lines:

O little town of Bethlehem, How still we see thee lie;
Above thy deep and dreamless sleep The silent stars go by.
Yet in thy dark streets shineth The everlasting light;
The hopes and fears of all the years Are met in thee to-
    night.

Five stanzas later (the original third stanza is omitted in today's hymnals), Brooks prayed that the Holy Child of Bethlehem would be born anew in each heart every Christmastime.

The following day when Mr. Lewis Redner (1831-1908), who was not only Church organist but also the Sunday School Superintendent, came into the minister's study, Brooks handed him a piece of paper on which he had written a copy of his new poem. "Lewis," he said to his friend and co-worker, "why not write a new tune for my poem. If it is a good tune, I will name it 'St. Lewis' after you."

Redner smiled as he glanced over the five stanzas and replied, "I will do what I can, Phillips, but if the music turns out to be a success, let us name it after you and call it 'St. Phillips.' "

Leaving the naming of the tune unsettled, Brooks urged Redner, a prominent Philadelphia business man as well as a leading Episcopalian layman, to do what he could as fast as he could, since the Christmas holiday was closer than "just around the corner." Although he had ample time in which to compose a suitable tune, Redner dabbled and delayed until it was almost too late. When Brooks pressed him, he gave the clergyman the age-old answer of frustrated composers, "No inspiration!" When he finally retired the night before Brooks had planned for a group of children to introduce the song, Redner had still not come up with a single line of music. But the hand of a beneficent Providence intervened to save the day, and Redner awoke during the night with a new tune ringing in his ears. He jotted down the melody as rapidly as he could and then went back to bed for a few hours of contented and undisturbed repose. Very early the next morning he harmonized his original melody and a group of six Sunday School teachers and thirty-six children sang it from newly printed leaflets on December 27, 1868.

Brooks paid his organist a worthy tribute without embarrassing him by naming the new tune "St. Louis," changing the spelling of the Superintendent's first name from "Lewis" to "Louis," an alteration which gave rise to many conjectures about a possible but non-existent connection between the mid-western city of that name and the name of the tune of the now-famous Christmas carol. Several years later, this hymn was included in "The Church Porch," but until it appeared in the official Hymnal of the Episcopal Church in 1892, the year before the poet's death, its use had been somewhat limited. However, following its initial publication in this Hymnal, it has grown in popularity and use and is now acclaimed one of the finest American carols in all the world.

The minister and his musician collaborated on another familiar Christmas song, "Everywhere, Everywhere Christmas Tonight," while Brooks is remembered for an equally beautiful Advent poem, the first line of which is, "The earth has grown cold with its burden of care."

After being consecrated Bishop of Massachusetts in October, 1891, Phillips Brooks lived only fifteen months, passing away on January 23, 1893, in his fifty-eighth year. The high esteem in which he was held by the children of his large parish is reflected in the words of a five-year-old girl who said to her mother, when told that Bishop Brooks had died, "Oh, Mother, how happy the angels will be!"

While Brooks and Redner remained bachelors all their lives, they lived to see the Christmas hymn in which they collaborated with such marked success become one of the favorites of children the world over. While any man can count himself fortunate if he is privileged to write a carol *or* a song *or* a poem that proved acceptable to his fellowmen, Brooks stands in a class all by himself for his carol (O Little Town Of Bethlehem), *and* his song (Everywhere, Everywhere Christmas Tonight) *and* his poem (The earth has grown cold with its burden of care) have become as much a part of Christmas as the tree, the holly and the mistletoe.

O LITTLE TOWN OF BETHLEHEM

O little town of Bethlehem, How still we see thee lie!
Above thy deep and dreamless sleep The silent stars go by;
Yet in thy dark streets shineth The everlasting Light;
The hopes and fears of all the years Are met in thee to-
      night.

For Christ is born of Mary, And gathered all above,
While mortals sleep, the angels keep Their watch of won-
      dering love.
O morning stars, together Proclaim the holy birth!
And praises sing to God the King, And peace to men on
      earth.

How silently, how silently, The wondrous gift is giv'n!
So God imparts to human hearts The blessings of his
      heav'n.

No ear may hear his coming, But in this world of sin,
Where meek souls will receive him, still The dear Christ
     enters in.

Where children pure and happy Pray to the blessed Child,
Where misery cries out to thee, Son of the mother mild;
Where charity stands watching And faith holds wide the
     door,
The dark night wakes, the glory breaks, And Christmas
     comes once more.

O holy Child of Bethlehem! Descend to us, we pray;
Cast out our sin and enter in, Be born in us today.
We hear the Christmas angels The great glad tidings tell;
O come to us, abide with us, Our Lord Immanuel.

EVERYWHERE, EVERYWHERE, CHRISTMAS TONIGHT

(This is the first of two stanzas)

  Everywhere, everywhere, Christmas tonight:
  Christmas in lands of the fir tree and pine;
  Christmas in lands of the palm tree and vine;
  Christmas where snow-peaks stand solemn and white;
  Christmas where cornfields lie sunny and bright;
  Everywhere, everywhere, Christmas tonight.

THE EARTH HAS GROWN COLD WITH ITS BURDEN OF CARE

(This is the first of four stanzas)

  The earth has grown cold with its burden of care,
  But at Christmas it always is young;
  The heart of the jewel burns lustrous and fair,
  And its soul full of music breaks forth on the air,
  When the song of the angels is sung.

Chapter **IX**

SILENT NIGHT

SILENT NIGHT

The combined efforts of five men and four children gave to Christendom her loveliest Christmas carol, "Silent Night." The first man was Father Joseph Mohr (1792-1848), assistant parish priest at the newly erected Church of St. Nicholas in Oberndorf, a relatively obscure village in the Austrian Alps, not too far from the city of Salzburg. Little dreaming that he was soon to write himself into immortality, Mohr listened intently as the second man, his Church organist, Franz Gruber (1787-1863) told him that the pipe organ in the Church would not be available for Midnight Mass on Christmas Eve, December 24, 1818, since it was broken almost beyond repair. At Mohr's insistence, thirty-one-year-old Gruber, who played the organ and trained the choir at nearby Arnsdorf in addition to his duties at Oberndorf, gave the instrument another thorough going-over before pronouncing it hopeless, whereupon the good Father, to relieve his inner tensions at the prospects of a Christmas Eve service without the traditional organ music, as well as to clear his mind and heart so as to be better able to cope with the unexpected emergency, bundled himself up in his warmest coat and set out to make several pastoral visits in some of the homes of his scattered mountain parish.

Gruber went back to the organ loft in a growing mood of despair and disappointment which is characteristic of musicians when they are thwarted or frustrated by ancient instruments that seem guaranteed to go to pieces on the eve of the most important religious services of the Christian year. With neither the time nor the talent, training, or tools to repair broken connections, restore and revoice antiquated pipes or replace a worn-out bellows, Gruber contented himself with pacing the floor, trying to dream up some solution to a problem that grew more critical with every passing hour.

Making the rounds of his parish with religious regularity, Father Mohr was suddenly summoned to the humble cottage of a poor woodcutter, to welcome as well as to bless a new born babe. On his way home that evening, Mohr contrasted and then compared the scene he had so recently witnessed with the birth of the Christ Child centuries ago in an humble stable behind the crowded inn at Bethlehem, and soon, to his surprise, he found himself creating a poem that was descriptive of the night on which both of the infants had been born.

The ideas that flooded his mind soon overcame

all thoughts of fatigue and weariness, while the parish priest hastened to the safety and security of his own little shelter in order to express his thoughts in poetic form. Soon, without too much conscious effort on his part, the words began to flow from his pen, and, as fast as he scratched them down on a piece of paper, other words and lines came crowding in to take their place. Before he knew it, he had penned several simple stanzas in a meter and mood that reflected true creative genius, entitling his poem, in his native German tongue, "Stille Nacht." As later translated into English, his first stanza read:

Silent night, Holy night, All is calm, all is bright;
Round yon Virgin Mother and Child, Holy Infant so
*   tender and mild,*
Sleep in heavenly peace, Sleep in heavenly peace.

When Franz Gruber burst into the room a few moments later and threw up his hands in complete disgust, Mohr refused to argue any further about the decrepit old pipe organ. Instead, he handed his friend a copy of his new stanzas. Then, going into the next room, he picked up a guitar, returning to place it in Gruber's hands with this admonition, "Franz, write some music for my new poem and we will sing it at Midnight Mass, organ or no organ."

When Gruber protested that he was an organist instead of a guitarist and a teacher rather than a composer, Mohr brushed his objections aside by explaining, "You surely know three chords on the guitar." As Gruber nodded affirmatively, the pastor continued, "Then write your music as simple as possible on those three chords, arrange it for two voices, and tonight while you play, we two will sing the new carol, and the service will be worthwhile if for no other reason than that the congregation will hear, for the first time, their minister and musician sing a vocal duet in public worship."

To quiet his friend, Gruber proceeded to do what he requested, and soon the two men were singing "Stille Nacht" to a melody that matched the spirit of the stanzas, while Gruber strummed the three chords on the guitar as an instrumental accompaniment. That historic night the song was sung publicly for the first time, receiving from the humble worshippers the acclaim it merited. And there the song might have remained had not the third man entered the scene in the early spring of the following year, 1819. He was Karl Mauracher, an organ builder and repairman from the valley of the Zillertal, who had finally received Gruber's letter and had come to fix the organ in the Church of St. Nicholas. When the instrument was in good playing order after days of back-breaking labor repairing, replacing or reworking every adjustable and move-

able part, Mauracher asked Gruber to try his
hand at it, and pass judgment on the work that
had been accomplished. Father Mohr happened
to be in the Church that afternoon and insisted
that the organist play the music he had composed
for the new Christmas carol several weeks earlier.
Although Gruber at first refused, at the urging
of the other two men he finally gave in and
played an organ arrangement of the music he
had picked out on the guitar some time before.
Mauracher immediately fell in love with the tune
and begged Gruber to give him a manuscript
copy of the new song. "I want to take it back
with me to the Zillertal Valley," he explained,
"and share it with the singers and musicians there
who are always on the lookout for a new song."

Gruber prepared the manuscript that very
evening, and when the organ builder bade the
two men "Goodbye" he took the carol with him,
wondering just who would be the right person
to give it to when he returned home. Ten years
were to pass before Mauracher found an answer
to the question that had been haunting him ever
since he had visited Oberndorf early in 1819, but
when he heard the four Strasser children singing
together he knew his search had come to an end.
He quickly arranged the new carol for four
children's voices, and, before long, Caroline,
Joseph, Andreas and Amalie Strasser were sing-

ing it as if it had been composed especially for them. "The four Strasser children sing like nightingales," the valley folk had said one to another for several months, but rarely did they sing in a more heavenly manner than when they joined their sweet voices in the stanzas of "Stille Nacht." Comments from people who soon learned to love the song as well as the singers, led the children to name it "The Song From Heaven."

With no idea that they were to be the means of introducing the carol to the world at large, the four children accompanied their parents to the great fair at Leipzig the following year, where Mr. and Mrs. Strasser offered their famous chamois-skin gloves for sale. To "drum up trade" the children sang in front of their parent's booth, and among those who stopped to listen was the fourth man of our story, the Director-General of Music of the Kingdom of Saxony, Mr. Pohlenz. He was so much impressed with the singing as well as the song that he invited the four Strassers to sing "The Song From Heaven" for the King and Queen in the Royal Saxon Court Chapel in Pleissenburg Castle the Christmas Eve of that very same year, 1832. The children and their song created a sensation, surpassed only by that which welcomed its rendition before King Frederick William IV

of Prussia twenty-two years later, an event which
inspired the monarch to express the desire that
"Stille Nacht" be given first place in all future
Christmas concerts within the bounds of his domain.

The part played by the fifth man did not come
to light until an Episcopalian rector from
Revere, Massachusetts, Rev. Byron Edward
Underwood, published an article in the October,
1957, issue of "The Hymn," the official publication of the Hymn Society of America, in which
he told the fascinating story of the Rev. John
Freeman Young (1820-1885), who was elected
Bishop of the Episcopalian Church in Florida
in 1867, identifying him as the man who had
translated Mohr's German poem into such flaw-
less, perfect English in 1863, four years prior
to his elevation to the Episcopacy. Until this
exhaustive and authentic article was printed,
hymnologists and poets had sought in vain for
the name of the person whose poetic skill had
placed all of English speaking and singing
Christendom in his debt.

"Silent Night" has taken its rightful place
among the most beautiful Christmas carols in all
the Christian world, thanks to the combined
labors of five men and four children and the
passing of time only adds new luster to its well-
deserved popularity and wide-spread use.

Silent Night

Silent night! holy night! All is calm, all is bright;
Round yon Virgin Mother and Child! Holy Infant, so
*   tender and mild,*
Sleep in heavenly peace, Sleep in heavenly peace.

Silent night! holy night! Shepherds quake at the sight,
Glories stream from heaven afar, Heavenly hosts sing
*   "Alleluia,*
Christ the Saviour is born, Christ the Saviour is born."

Silent night! holy night! Son of God, love's pure Light
Radiant beams from Thy holy face, With the dawn of re-
*   deeming grace,*
Jesus, Lord, at Thy birth, Jesus, Lord, at Thy birth.

Silent night! holy night! Wondrous Star, lend thy light;
With the angels let us sing, Alleluia to our King;
Christ the Saviour is born, Christ the Saviour is born.

Chapter X

THE FIRST NOEL

THE FIRST NOEL

The origin of the word "noel," and even its exact original meaning, like so many other words that have grown up with the English language, seem lost in the mists of antiquity. Like many other words that achieve popularity, it came to be claimed by several tongues, and to be ascribed numerous derivations.

For example, some scholars claim the word is of French origin, signifying "a shout of joy" at the birth of the baby Jesus, while others, pressing further back into the medieval Latin, say it is derived from a familiar word "natalis" which means "birth," having to do with the birth of our Lord; hence we speak of Christmas as "His natal day." Then there is another Latin word that some claim as the real grandfather of "noel," the word "novella" which means "news" conveying the idea that the news of the coming of Christ caused the shouts of joy associated with the Advent season.

To complicate matters even further, one or two linguists see a close connection between a corruption of the Latin "natalis" into the Provençal "nadal." But how that resulted in "noel" is a mystery, the missing linguistic link never having been discovered. More than likely, the correct English spelling of the word is "nowell" rather than the French "noël," with the umlaut over the "ë." That being true, it would not take an historian very long to figure out that this is another example of the English talent for abbreviation. For example, around the year 1247 A.D. a hospital was founded in England and given the name "St. Mary of Bethlehem." Several centuries after its establishment, this hospital was turned into an asylum for the insane, and the noise and confusion associated with such an institution in bygone days became known, not only throughout the surrounding countryside but also throughout the length and breadth of England. Thus it came to pass that the ancestors of Chaucer and Shakespeare corrupted and contracted "St. Mary of Bethlehem" into a new word "Bedlam," and the word "bedlam," spelled with a small "b," soon became synonymous with unorganized confusion and all of the shouts, cries, screams, yells and assorted noises that issue from an insane asylum.

In quite the same way, the English people took the delightful parting phrase with which our ancestors bade one another "Farewell," the phrase "God be with you," and, tiring of its length, or mouthing it too quickly or half-swallowing it, corrupted and contracted the four words into one, the word "Goodbye," just as they had taken "Fare thee well" and made it into one word also.

Undoubtedly the word "nowell" was at first a phrase instead of a word, and of all the phrases that it could be expanded into, none is more appropriate than the four words "Now all is well!" Therefore it seems both reasonable and possible that our forefathers greeted each other every Christmas morning with the cry "Now all is well" since Christ had come and since God had regarded those who had walked in darkness by giving them a great light. When pessimistic unbelievers ranted and raved about "what the world had come to," Christians replied with their optimistic observation about Him "who had come into the world." "Now all is well" soon became merely "Now well," and it was a short step from those two words to the one word "Nowell," and this explanation is no more fanciful than that "St. Mary of Bethlehem" should become, within the span of a few centuries, such a word as "bedlam."

So, when the unknown poet who wrote "The First Nowell" sat down to compose his narrative poem about the birth of Jesus sometime during the seventeenth century, he decided that the message of the angels to the shepherds, "Fear not, for behold I bring you good tidings of great joy which shall be to all people" (Luke 2:10), was a message to remind them that "now all is well" for Christ is born in Bethlehem, that being the "first" of the "nowells" Christians have said to one another each succeeding Christmas. For us of this century, the same message to others of our own generation would be "the two-thousandth nowell," since the age-old song of the angels has lost none of its grandeur or its glory with the passing of twenty centuries.

The anonymous poet and the unknown minstrel who composed the music did a thorough job of their composition, because their Christmas carol has been a popular one for almost three centuries, and is about the oldest familiar carol in the English language. Despite the fact that the poet took some liberties with the New Testament story, such as having the shepherds look up and see the star, and numbering the "wise men" by the number of their gifts, he did have the intelligence to remind believers of his day that the infant Jesus grew into manhood to become the Christ "who with His blood mankind hath bought," thus linking the mystery of His birth with the mystery of His death.

"The First Nowell" is an excellent example of the kind of song Christians began to sing when the Roman Catholic Church relegated all singing to the trained choir, denying the people the privilege of raising their voices together in praise of God. When they were refused permission to sing inside their Churches and Cathedrals, these Christians went outside and sang and danced to their heart's content. To accompany their joyous dances, they created simple and lilting tunes for which wandering minstrels quickly supplied appropriate verses. Following the Protestant Reformation, congregational singing once more became the vogue, with the father of the movement, Martin Luther himself, not only leading the singing but writing words and music of his own for use in such services of public worship. It was at that time that many of the popular secular songs were polished up and made suitable for use inside the Churches, and became the beloved religious folk-songs of the people.

A "carol" is technically "a round or ring dance," the word being derived from "carola," and originally referred more to one who accompanied the dancers on the flute or another musical instrument, rather than to the song itself. Later, as better stanzas were prepared for the dancers and the on-lookers to sing, the word came to apply more to the verses than the dances. Thus it became synonymous with a song of exaltation and mirth or a joyous ballad of praise, devotion and thanksgiving to God for the gift of Jesus at Christmastime.

In striking contrast to the doleful "plain song" and the monotonous ancient chants, the carols were excitingly gay and cheerful. Thus they were used and loved by the people far more than those hymns and chants that had received the pontifical approval of ecclesiastical authorities in Rome, Athens or Jerusalem. "The First Nowell," after having been handed down by word-of-voice for many generations, was finally copied down with the stanzas properly polished and the tune correctly harmonized, and printed for the first time in a collection of Christmas carols published in 1833. From that volume it has sung its way into the hymnals of the universal Church and rare indeed is the Christmas when the "Refrain" "Nowell, Nowell, Nowell, Nowell, Born is the King of Israel" is not heard throughout Christendom.

In like manner, the perennially popular French carol "Angels We Have Heard On High" with its lilting "Chorus" "Gloria In Excelsis Deo" (Glory to God in the highest) is also anonymous, the name of both poet and composer being unrecorded anywhere. More than likely it sprung up in France about the same time and in the same way that "The First Nowell" developed in Britain.

"Good Christian Men, Rejoice" (In Dulci Jubilo) from a Latin poet of the Middle Ages and a fourteenth century German composer, is another splendid example of an anonymous carol that has lasted through the centuries because of its message and appeal.

Every one of these Christmas hymns, whether their authors and composers are known or unknown, remind believers of all ages that it is more important to know that Christ has come than to know the name of the individual who created the stanzas or prepared the music of a particular Christmas hymn. Suffice it to say, in a paraphrase of the epitaph on the gravestone of the great Rev. Isaac Watts, "Ages unborn will make these songs, The joy and labor of their tongues."

THE FIRST NOEL

The first Noel the angel did say
Was to certain poor shepherds in fields as they lay;
In fields as they lay keeping their sheep,
On a cold winter's night that was so deep.
    Noel, Noel, Noel, Noel;
    Born is the King of Israel.

They looked up and saw a star
Shining in the east, beyond them far,
And to the earth it gave great light,
And so it continued both day and night.

And by the light of that same star,
Three wise men came from country far;
To seek for a King was their intent,
And to follow the star wherever it went.

This star drew nigh to the north-west;
O'er Bethlehem it took its rest,
And there it did both stop and stay
Right over the place where Jesus lay.

Then entered in those wise men three
Full reverently upon the knee,
And offered there in his presence
Their gold and myrrh and frankincense.

Then let us all with one accord
Sing praises to our heavenly Lord,
That hath made heaven and earth of nought,
And with his blood mankind hath bought.

Chapter XI

THERE'S A SONG IN THE AIR

THERE'S A SONG IN THE AIR

If any popular Christmas carol deserves to be called "The New England Carol" it is "There's A Song In The Air," because both the author of the words, poet-novelist Josiah Gilbert Holland (1819-1881) and composer Karl Pomeroy Harrington (1861-1953) were in New England when they played their particular parts in this lovely song's interesting history.

While we do not know if Holland penned his words in mid-winter, we do know that Harrington composed his music in mid-summer, the least likely time for a musician to be inspired to write a Christmas tune. Poet Holland, a one-time high school drop-out because of poor health, tried his hand successively at photography and calligraphy before enrolling in a medical school. After earning his degree and practicing his profession for a few years, he forsook medicine to become the owner and editor of a newspaper. Apparently he "found himself" in the world of letters, "the fourth estate," because he remained a writer, poet, novelist and editor until his death. It was in his book "The Marble Prophecy And Other Poems," published in 1872, that the four stanzas of "There's A Song In The Air" ap-

peared in print for the first time. They proved
to be so popular with his readers that he included
them in his 1879 publication "Complete Poetical
Writings."

Holland wrote his poem in four six-line stanzas, arranged in a most unusual manner. The
first four lines of each stanza contained six syllables each, while the fifth and sixth lines contained
twelve syllables each, a metrical pattern desig-
nated 6.6.6.6.12.12. This is the only example of
this particular metrical pattern in contemporary
hymnody. Critics may say that the poet should
have cut his last two twelve-syllable lines in half,
and written his stanzas in eight lines of six syllables each instead, but he wrote it the way he
wanted to, which is always a poet's privilege, although it made the poem all the more difficult to
set to singable music.

A little over thirty years after Holland first
published his carol, it attracted the attention of a
scholarly university Latin teacher and part-time
musician, Professor Karl P. Harrington. Where
he discovered the stanzas or under what circum-
stances, the composer never said. He did reveal,
however, the interesting incidents connected with
his composition. Harrington came from a very
musical and creative family. His father before
him had been one of the musical editors of a
Methodist Hymnal, and, quite early in his life,
young Karl had tried his hand at composing

hymn tunes on the small Estey organ which stood in the living room of the Harrington home in Middletown. Many years later, when Karl had grown to man's estate and had purchased a summer cottage for his own family at North Woodstock, New Hampshire, his father decided it was time to purchase a new and larger parlor organ for the old home place. When the new instrument was delivered, he gave the small Estey to Karl, who promptly moved it to his North Woodstock vacation retreat. While spending some time there in July, 1904, on a sudden impulse he sat at the keyboard of the old Estey organ, for which, he confessed, he had developed "a sentimental fondness," pumped up the bellows with the foot pedals, and then and there proceeded to compose his lovely melodic tune for Holland's stirring stanzas.

In the Preface to the 1905 edition of The Methodist Hymnal is a list of the Bishops of the participating Churches, the names of the members of the Commission appointed by these Bishops and this note, "On recommendation of the Joint Commission of the General Conferences of The Methodist Episcopal Church, and The Methodist Episcopal Church, South, Professor Karl P. Harrington of Wesleyan University and Professor Peter C. Lutkin of Northwestern University were appointed musical editors." Thus it came to pass that Harrington's most popular sacred compositions and Lutkin's best musical creations appeared in print for the first time in this particular edition of The Methodist Hymnal. In fact, this 1905 collection contained fourteen original tunes by Harrington and nineteen by Lutkin.   Professor Lutkin later admitted that the committee found itself so short of tunes at the very last moment that he dashed off several with almost reckless abandon in order to fill the pages of the proposed hymnal by the publication deadline.

Of Lutkin's nineteen tunes, two have survived after the passing of half a century: the tune "Lanier," for Sidney Lanier's only claim to hymnic fame, "Into The Woods My Master Went" and the beautiful choral setting for "The Lord Bless You And Keep You" (Numbers 6:24–26) which became so deservedly popular that it is known today simply as "Lutkin's Benediction."

As for his co-worker, Professor Harrington, he too has only two of his fourteen original tunes in common usage today: the music for the carol, "There's A Song In The Air," and his musical setting for another familiar Old Testament passage, Habakkuk 2:20, "The Lord Is In His Holy Temple, Let All The Earth Keep Silence Before Him."   Interestingly enough, many Church services in our own day open with Harrington and close with Lutkin.

Another composition for a Christmas hymn by Harrington also appeared in print for the first time in this 1905 Hymnal, a musical setting for Episcopal Bishop Leigh Richmond Brewer's hymn "Long Years Ago O'er Bethlehem's Hills Was Seen A Wondrous Thing." This carol came into existence in a most remarkable manner. When Brewer was serving as the Episcopal Bishop of Montana, a wealthy friend responded to his appeal for financial assistance by sending him a check for $5,000. In gratitude to this friend for his generous gift, the Bishop penned this poem just before Christmas of that same year, 1892, and sent it to the donor as a personal Christmas greeting. In the 1905 Hymnal, there are three musical settings for Holland's Christmas poem and two for Brewer's. In both instances, Harrington's are listed as "second tunes." The first tunes in both cases came from the prolific pen of a now unknown composer, Alfred George Wathall. This native of Nottingham, England, who had been brought to the United States as a child, was written up in the Companion to the Hymnal as "possibly the youngest composer represented in this book." But even at that, the editor stated that the seven original tunes in the book were not Wathall's first hymn tunes, and added, "All seven tunes were composed within an hour's time. Although many of our great hymns and tunes have been written in a few moments, we know of nothing that equals this for speed of composition." Today we search in vain to find Wathall in a contemporary hymnal, while Harrington and Lutkin go singing on!

Composer Harrington aptly named his tune "Christmas Song." While both words, "Christmas" and "Song" had been used singly or in other combinations in connection with different Advent hymns, this was the first time they had been wedded in this manner. The hymn tune "Christmas" is the tune to which Nahum Tate's carol, "While Shepherds Watched Their Flocks By Night" (as well as Doddridge's hymn "Awake My Soul, Stretch Every Nerve"), is sung. This music was adapted from a melody composed in 1728 by Handel for his opera "Siroe." While poet Tate was called "a man of intemperate and improvident habits," in striking contrast, composer Handel "died as he lived, a good Christian, with a true sense of his duty to God and man, and in perfect charity to all the world." As prolific a composer as Handel was, he only composed three hymn tunes as such, and did them at the personal request of Charles Wesley who had met the renowned composer in the home of a mutual British friend.

The tune named "Christmas Hymn," composed for John Byrom's poem, "Christians, Awake! Salute The Happy Morn," is more often entitled "Yorkshire"; while the tune named "Christmas Carol" is assigned to Sir H. Walford Davies' music for Phillips Brooks' "O Little Town Of Bethlehem," when he was requested to compose a new musical setting by Rev. Garrett Horder in 1905 for a new British song book.

So we have tunes named "Christmas," "Christmas *Hymn*," "Christmas *Song*," and "Christmas *Carol*." To top it all off, Harrington named his tune for Bishop Brewer's poem "Christmas *Eve*" but he didn't have the heart to let it stand that way in print, because he translated the words into German and the music, composed in 1903, now bears the name "Weihnacht."

Speaking of these hymn tune names, Charles Wesley's "Hark, The Herald Angels Sing" is as fine a Christmas *hymn* as has ever been written, a hymn being "a religious poem, written to be sung, that is addressed to or is descriptive of one of the Persons of the Holy Trinity: The Father, The Son, or The Holy Spirit (Ghost)." "There's A Song In The Air" qualifies as a splendid Christmas *carol,* despite the name the composer gave to his music; while such perennial favorites as James Pierpont's "Jingle Bells" and Irving Berlin's "White Christmas" are classified as Christmas *songs.*

In the United States, the Episcopalians have produced more Christmas hymns and carols than any of the other denominations: Bishop Brooks' stanzas "O Little Town Of Bethlehem," coupled with Episcopalian Sunday School Superintendent and Church Organist Lewis Redner's tune "St. Louis"; and Rev. John Henry Hopkins' words and music for "We Three Kings Of Orient Are." Katherine Lee Bates, of "America The Beautiful" fame, and author of the Christmas carol "The Kings Of The East Are Riding" was the daughter of a Congregational minister; Rev. Edmund Sears, a Unitarian, wrote "It Came Upon The Midnight Clear." Professor Karl P. Harrington, a leading layman, apparently the only American Methodist to make an enduring contribution to Christmas hymnody, composed the tune, "Christmas Song" for Josiah G. Holland's poem, "There's A Song In The Air."

There's a Song in the Air

There's a song in the air!
  There's a star in the sky!
There's a mother's deep prayer,
  And a baby's low cry!
And the star rains its fire while the beautiful sing,
For the manger of Bethlehem cradles a King!

There's a tumult of joy
  O'er the wonderful birth,
For the Virgin's sweet boy
  Is the Lord of the earth.
Ay! the star rains its fire while the beautiful sing,
For the manger of Bethlehem cradles a King!

In the light of that star
  Lie the ages impearled;
And that song from afar
  Has swept over the world.
Every hearth is aflame, and the beautiful sing
In the homes of the nations that Jesus is King!

We rejoice in the light,
  And we echo the song
That comes down through the night
  From the heavenly throng.
Ay! we shout to the lovely evangel they bring,
And we greet in his cradle, our Saviour and King!

Chapter *XII*

WE THREE KINGS OF ORIENT ARE

WE THREE KINGS OF ORIENT ARE

This popular Christmas hymn that some people do not consider a carol or a hymn at all was first published in the author's own volume, "Carols, Hymns And Songs," a book that went through three editions from 1862 to 1882. While some authorities date the words and music of this particular hymn as early as 1857, the poet-composer's thirty-seventh year, its first publication was in the first edition of the afore-mentioned collection of original poems in 1862. The reason some hymnologists refuse to recognize this carol as a Christian hymn is because, to them, it perpetuates a falsehood. These folk are of the opinion that while the Bible does speak of "wise men from the east" travelling to worship the new-born King, it does not say authoritatively that these wanderers were Kings. So to sing a Christmas hymn about Kings who were not Kings is to sing something that, in the words of a popular song, "ain't necessarily so!" But that problem, important or insignificant as it may be, did not trouble Rev. John Henry Hopkins, Jr., when he wanted to write his carol about the visit of the wise men. Whether they were actually wise men or Magi or Magicians or Kings seemed of secondary importance to the fact that some very noble personages from a far away country did make the long and perilous trip to Jerusalem and on to Bethlehem, there to worship Him whom the angels called "A Saviour, who is Christ the Lord."

While the Biblical accounts give a great many hints as to their identity, the four Gospel writers never come out and say exactly who they were or precisely where they came from. Some translators of the Bible claim that they were astrologers, and render the original Greek into English by means of that word. Astrology (literally: star-discourse) the so-called science which treats of the influences of the stars and planets on human affairs, and the art of foretelling human events by the movements, positions, aspects and relative relationships of the heavenly bodies, is not to be confused with Astronomy (literally: star-regulate), which is the science which treats of the heavenly bodies themselves with regard to their size, motions, constitution, orbits and relationships to other heavenly bodies.

In ancient times, the Magi were a priestly caste or cult in Media and Persia, who not only dabbled in astrology but also in sorcery, which dealt with the use of power gained supposedly from the help of evil spirits, and was closely akin to necromancy, the art of revealing the future by communication with the spirits of the departed. Claiming power over the living as well as the dead, they conjured up their miracles and kept the people in their power by means of their astounding magic.

Now, whether the "three kings" were really philosophers, wise men, astrologers, sorcerers, Magi or Monarchs, we will never know for an absolute certainty. Suffice it to say that they knew the movements of the stars and read in them what men of lesser learning overlooked or ignored. The three names that tradition gave to the kings, Caspar, Melchior and Balthasar, were chosen somewhere along the way, while the number three was selected because of the three gifts: gold, frankincense and myrrh, since it was suggested that each man brought one special gift with him to lay at the feet of the infant Jesus.

Travellers throughout the deserts and mountain fastnesses of oriental Asia never take long journeys in small groups, especially when bearing "costly gifts so rare" because they would be facing certain death at the hands of marauding robber bands that have infested that portion of the world for countless generations. More than likely, a huge retinue made the long and dangerous trip to Jerusalem, whether from Persia, Arabia, Chaldaea, Babylonia, Mesopotamia or India, for a safe arrival at such a distant destination demanded a large group for mutual protection against wild nomads as well as organized gangs of cut-throats and thieves.

In fact, it is unlikely that Herod the King would have paid any attention to three camel-borne easterners, no matter how well garbed they were or how regally they rode their "ships of the desert" into his capital city. A larger group, however, would have caused consternation in Jerusalem and compelled Herod to take notice of their arrival within the boundaries of his domain. The fact that "Herod was troubled and all Jerusalem with him" (Matthew 2:3) proves the likelihood of this theory. Otherwise, he would not have bothered himself with their questions regarding a star in the east, and a new-born King of the Jews whom they had come such a distance to adore. But Herod was troubled; in fact, he was frightened almost out of his wits! So, assembling the chief priests and the scribes, he demanded to know more, even summoning the strange visitors to his palace to ascertain from them in person the exact time of the appearance of the unusual astral spectacle. Undoubtedly these remarkable men came from a land that was long familiar with the Hebrew Scriptures, and were themselves steeped in the lore of the five books of Moses. For in Numbers 24:17 this prophecy appears, "A star shall come forth out of Jacob and a scepter shall rise out of Israel," the star in the heavens and the scepter, which is always the sign of a King, being mentioned in the very same passage and almost in the very same breath. No one but a seeker after truth who knew these Old Testament words and promises would have left the security of an eastern palace to travel for many months over uncharted territory to an unknown country, braving untold dangers in order to present unrequested gifts to an uncrowned king!

But come they did, worshipping the baby Jesus in his house in the City of David (Matthew 2:11) sometime after his birth in a stable not too far away, and presenting him the gifts they had journeyed so far and so long to give. Had it not been for that gift of gold, Joseph and Mary could hardly have afforded the expense involved in their sudden and unexpected flight into Egypt, when Herod, having been tricked by the wise men who returned to their country another way without reporting to him in Jerusalem, sought to lay his hands upon the future king, and, in his wrath, ordered the death of every male child two years of age and under in and around the town of Bethlehem. Thus was the providence of God at work through devious ways to protect His Son from the cruel designs of an unscrupulous ruler.

If they were truly Kings, rarely have Kings shown better judgment, and if they were merely wise men, then they deserved to be Kings because of their brilliance, foresight, faith, courage and daring, qualities sadly lacking in many whose brows have been adorned with a jewelled crown.

So the Episcopalian rector was not far from wrong in beginning his hymn with these lines:

We three Kings of Orient are, Bearing gifts we traverse afar,
Field and fountain, moor and mountain, Following yonder star.
Oh, star of wonder, star of night, Star with royal beauty bright;
Westward leading, still proceeding, Guide us to thy perfect light.

If it takes a King to recognize a King, these men qualify, because, of all the thousands who crowded the narrow streets of the Holy City that first Christmas Eve, they alone saw in the baby Jesus the King God intended Him to be! In their choices of gifts they could not have exercised better judgment, for gold always signifies the presence of a ruling monarch, while frankincense "owns a deity nigh" and myrrh, which was used for the embalming of the dead, foretold "the gathering gloom" of Calvary's cross.

But Hopkins (1820-1891) was not content with just telling the story of the visit of the wise men. Unlike many poets, this native American hymn-writer looked beyond Christmas to Good Friday and to Easter Sunday and sang:

Glorious now behold Him arise, King and God and Sacrifice;
Alleluia, Alleluia, Sounds through the earth and skies.

Setting his own poem to music, this distinguished son of an honored Bishop of the Episcopalian Church in Vermont wrote himself into immortality with one of the rare carols that some folks refuse to admit is a carol at all, but which dramatizes in a splendid way the Scriptural account of the visit of the wise men to the infant Jesus.

Although Hopkins published two other collections of poems, some of which contained hymns that eventually found their way into several hymnals after the poet's passing in 1891, this Christmas hymn alone has earned the universal applause it so well merited, for it possessed the universal appeal that is guaranteed to keep it alive until the Kings of this world confess the Lordship of Him whom God sent to be the King of Kings and the Lord of Lords.

WE THREE KINGS OF ORIENT ARE

We three kings of orient are,
Bearing gifts we traverse afar,
Field and fountain, moor and mountain,
Following yonder star.
> *O star of wonder, star of night,*
> *Star with royal beauty bright;*
> *Westward leading, still proceeding,*
> *Guide us to thy perfect light!*

Born a King on Bethlehem's plain,
Gold I bring to crown him again,
King forever, ceasing never
Over us all to reign.

Frankincense to offer have I;
Incense owns a Deity nigh;
Prayer and praising all men raising,
Worship him, God on high.

Myrrh is mine; its bitter perfume
Breathes a life of gathering gloom;
Sorrowing, sighing, bleeding, dying,
Sealed in a stone-cold tomb.

Glorious now behold him arise,
King and God and Sacrifice;
Alleluia, Alleluia!
Sounds through the earth and skies.

Chapter XIII

CAROLS OF ALL NATIONS

CAROLS OF ALL NATIONS

Carols of All Nations

When Christmas time approaches and familiar carols ring,
The peoples of the world march in, each with a song to
sing;
I think the Heavenly Father planned that it should be this
way,
To bind a broken, shattered world in one, each Christmas
Day.

The Englishman, George Handel, joins with Isaac Watts
to sing
"Joy to the world, the Lord is come, Let earth receive her
King."
While Frenchman Adolphe Adam the organ's chambers
swell,
To play a matchless melody, his "Cantique de Noel."

The British sing their rousing carol, driving gloom away,
"God rest ye merry, gentlemen, Let nothing you dismay";
While Welshmen, gath'ring round the board, in festive mood
and jolly,
Unite to swell the chorus, "Deck the halls with boughs of
holly."

"The First Noel" from Britain and "Torches Bring" from
France;
"It Came Upon the Midnight Clear" from a Unitarian
manse.

The Italian poet, Christina Rossetti, gives the rhyme,
"Love came down at Christmas, Love all lovely, Love
  Divine."

Phillips Brooks, Bostonian, now lifts his voice on high,
"O Little Town Of Bethlehem, How still we see thee lie;"
While unknown ancient Latins the same old story tell
In "Adeste Fidelis" and "Veni Immanuel."

The Polish children sing a song as lovely as them all,
"Infant holy, infant lowly, for his bed a cattle stall";
While other children sing a lovely lullaby instead,
The lilting "Away in a manger, no crib for a bed."

The humble poor of every land sing all the world around,
"While shepherds watched their flocks by night all seated
  on the ground";
And "Angels from the realms" and "As with gladness men
  of old,"
While "We Three Kings Of Orient" the guiding star behold.

We "Hail To The Lord's Annointed" "In dulci jubilo,"
While Frenchmen sing their "Gloria in excelsis Deo";
And "Good King Wenceslaus" looks out to see the wonders
  there,
While Americans are carolling "There's A Song In The
  Air."

For Charles Wesley, Methodist, the heavenly anthems
  ring,
With Mendelssohn, the Jew, in "Hark, The Herald Angels
  Sing";
While Mohr and Gruber, Austrians, put darkness all to
  flight,
And sing for us the universal fav'rite, "Silent Night."

Around the throne of God we'll join and sing these songs
    one day,
With "every kindred, every tribe" when earth has passed
    away.
We'll "hail the power of Jesus' Name" while "angels
    prostrate fall,
Bring forth the royal diadem and crown Him Lord of all.' "

Ernest K. Emurian is the author of more than fifteen books, including several on hymn stories (see page 2 for a list). He has himself composed hymns and semipopular songs. He is a graduate of Davidson College (A.B.), Union Theological Seminary in Virginia (B.D.), and Princeton Theological Seminary (Th.M.), and has served several pastorates.